CHRISTOPHER WALKEN

MOVIE TOP TEN

CREDITS

CHRISTOPHER WALKEN: MOVIE TOP TEN
Edited by Jack Hunter
ISBN 1 871592 84 4
© Creation Books & individual contributors 1999
Creation Movie Top Tens: a periodical, review-based publication
First published 2000 by:
Creation Books International
Design/layout/typesetting:
Bradley Davis, PCP International
Cover illustration:
"The Dead Zone"

Photo credits:
All photos are authorized publicity stills, by courtesy of the BFI, London; Kobal Collection, London; MOMA, New York; and the Jack Hunter Collection.

Copyright acknowledgements:
Every reasonable effort has been made to trace the owners of copyright materials in this book, but in some instances this has proven impossible. The editor and publishers will be glad to receive information leading to more complete acknowledgements in subsequent printings of the book, and in the meantime extend their apologies for any omissions.

British Library Cataloguing in Publication Data:
A catalogue record for this book is available from the British Library

A Butcherbest Production

Creation Books
"Popular books for popular people"

www.creationbooks.com

CONTENTS

INTRODUCTION
IMPRESSIONS OF DARKNESS

I don't need to be made to look evil. I can do that on my own.
—Christopher Walken[1]

Perhaps the defining career moment for Christopher Walken in recent years would come, ironically, when he was nowhere to be seen. During the 1997 Oscars ceremony, acclaimed character actor Kevin Spacey, on stage to hand out a statue, seized the opportunity to launch into an amusing and near perfect impersonation. It was a small but significant moment. In front of the who's who of Tinseltown's major players and a global viewing audience into the billions, Christopher Walken – the personification of the edgy, oozing-with-cerebral-menace anti-Hollywood hero – finally had his slab-black image crystallised for the world.

With his gravity-defying hair, calculating nonchalant voice, deeply ambiguous smile and that incinerated, waxen, reptilian visage, there is an otherworldly alienness about Christopher Walken. It is this troubling combination of distinctive genetics, chilly sexuality and twitching mannerisms that – distilled into the re-windable permanency of celluloid – has turned him into a genuine, cult movie star. But he's no chiselled icon in the heart-throb Willis, Cage, Gibson, Connery, Ford mould, a ceaseless procession of wallet imploding paychecks, tabloid inches and magazine covers. His idiosyncratic looks and NY gangster-style vocals would render that career path impossible from the start. Rather, the light comes from an evil, often dazzling glow that emanates from Walken onscreen, however sinister, psychotic or sadistic his character.

The background to Spacey's Oscar night impersonation remains incomplete. For Walken, who has perpetually flirted with the Dark Side in countless film personas, how improbable then, that director George Lucas had him as his second choice for the role of Han Solo in the original **Star Wars** (the part ultimately taken by the then virtually unknown Harrison Ford). Spacey, privy to this fascinating morsel of film esoterica had, prior to the Oscars skit, done a classic sketch mimicking Walken auditioning for **Star Wars** for the groundbreaking comedy show *Saturday Night Live*.

This near miss in casting terms – and with hindsight, how incalculably different **Star Wars** might have been – has hardly dented the Walken career however. A self-confessed workaholic, his curriculum vitae is now considerable (60 films and rising) and since the mid-1980s he has often appeared in four or five films a year.

I can say no to hardly any role. I don't have children and I don't have hobbies. I don't like to travel really. I like to stay in the house unless I'm working. So it's better for me psychologically.[2]

Yet the more high profile films roles have been in artistic conjunction with a number of the most daring, innovative, left-of-centre directors of the last two decades – including Tim Burton, Abel Ferrara, David Cronenberg, James Foley and Paul Schrader. Walken has also appeared in more mainstream Hollywood productions too, as his bad guy performances in money-spinning film franchises including the Bond film **A View To A Kill** (1985), **Batman Returns** (1992) – where as Max Shreck, he takes delight in throwing Michelle Pfeiffer out of a window – and **Wayne's World 2** (1993) testify.

Walken's prolific filmography suggests that he considers himself no more than an actor for hire and has no artistic pretensions towards any particular film genre (or any noticeable desires towards superstardom). Inevitably, he has seen his share of critical and commercial failures. On the subject he has simply said, "I make a lot of movies. I don't really have anything else to do. Some of them go straight to video. They're so obscure. I make movies that nobody will see. I've made a number of movies that I have never seen..."[3] and "...I don't make career choices. I just take the next best job. I save my money. I'm very very careful."[4]

Born Ronald Walken in March 1943 in New York, Walken was the third son (with Glenn and Ken) of a German baker father and an ambitious, stage-struck Scottish mother. The family owned a bakery in the working-class suburb of Queens. The young Walken, at his mother's urging, would attend a professional children's school, work briefly, aged fifteen, as a lion tamer and would spend much of the 1950s working as a child actor during the golden era of live TV, making appearances with legends including Milton Berle, Jerry Lewis and Dean Martin. He made his Broadway debut aged sixteen and enjoyed a short-lived but highly praised career in musicals until, aged twenty-five, he decided to change his name.

The following year, it would be in **Me And My Brother** (1968) that Walken would land his first film role. It was also the year of his marriage to Georgianne, a casting agent. They met as dancers in small-time musicals during his Broadway tenure. Their marriage continues to the present – in the neurotic insecurities of the US film industry, a considerable rarity. The Sean Connery vehicle **The Anderson Tapes** followed three years later but he would have to wait another five years for his next feature, as a poet in **Next Stop Greenwich Village** (1976). There would then be critical praise for his performance in director James Ivory's **Roseland** (1977). But it was his other performance of that year, in Woody Allen's classic **Annie Hall** – Walken cast in a cameo role as Diane Keaton's auto-destructive brother Duane Hall who takes Allen for a terrifying drive in the country – which would hint at the embryonic beginnings of his career to follow.

Walken would capitalise on his modest success in **Annie Hall** almost immediately and with his next film, achieve the greatest critical plaudits of his career to date. Casting him alongside Robert De Niro, Meryl Street, John Cazale and John Savage, director/writer Michael Cimino's **The Deer Hunter** (1978) was an epic film about the effects of war on the human soul. Walken was cast as Nick, a young factory steel worker from Pennsylvania who with his friends Michael (De Niro) and Steven (Savage) experience the savageries of the Vietnam war.

Beautifully filmed, acted and written, Walken's charged performance remains a remarkable portrait of disintegration and destruction, not least during the now infamous Russian Roulette sequence, a uniquely harrowing and seminal scene in modern cinema. Walken would pick up a Best Supporting Actor Oscar, a Bafta and other awards, so mesmeric was his complex portrayal of incandescent desolation.

That roulette scene in particular had a powerful effect on the sort of parts I did afterwards. It left an impression of darkness that stuck.[5]

Celebrity status inevitably followed and soon Walken was to briefly enjoy the limelight with, among others, the famously hard-living comic actor John Belushi and icon of kitsch art Andy Warhol. Yet his status onscreen was far from cemented. Though he took the lead role in John Irving's **The Dogs Of War** (1980), his reteaming with director Cimino for the now legendary **Heaven's Gate** the following year, proved disastrous for all concerned. A vast, sprawling western, the isolated location and the director's crippling perfectionism saw the budget spiral uncontrollably from $8m to $38m (nearly bringing about the financial demise of United Artists). Creating barely a flicker at the box office, **Heaven's Gate** was to become one of the most expensive flops in cinema history. Though he only appeared in a cameo role as Nate Champion, it was a misplaced performance (his ghostly pallor seems startlingly incongruous in all that open air ("I don't like the feel of it [the sun] on my skin..") and Walken's career temporarily went into freefall.

Partly redeeming himself as a dazzling dancer in **Pennies From Heaven** (1981), in essence a return to his Broadway song and dance days, two years would pass before he took lead roles in both **Brainstorm** and **The Dead Zone**. Directed by special effects supremo Douglas Trumbull (who created the spectacular space sequences in Stanley Kubrick's **2001**), **Brainstorm** co-starred Louise Fletcher, the Oscar-winning actress from **One Flew Over The Cuckoo's Nest** in a sci-fi thriller about a sensory experience device with explosive cerebral capabilities. Shot partly in the 70mm format,

much of its impact is dramatically reduced on TV and video. Filming however, would be overshadowed by the tragic death of Walken's co-star Natalie Wood who drowned one night following a late night dive from her yacht in which she, Walken and her husband Robert Wagner had been partying. The shadow Wood's death was to cast over the film would affect everyone and though Walken would immerse himself in his work immediately, the negative publicity and rumours surrounding the incident would continue for some time. He would effectively end the cultivation of a public private life from the completion of **Brainstorm** onwards.

Later in the year, master of the twisted imagination David Cronenberg (**Crash, Dead Ringers, The Fly**) cast Walken as a psychic foreseer in **The Dead Zone** (1983), a man who sees terrifying visions of the future. Based on novelists Stephen King's bestseller, in a neat real-life twist in the tale, after making references to the story *The Legend Of Sleepy Hollow* in the film, sixteen years later, Walken would make a small cameo appearance in Tim Burton's own film version of the dark text in **Sleepy Hollow** (1999).

Two years would pass before his next film role in **A View To A Kill** (1985), playing Max Zorin, arch nemesis of the aging Roger Moore (it was his last outing) as the suave epitome of the ruthless spy. With his hair dyed a lurid yellow and actress/villain Grace Jones at his side (and stealing much of the limelight), it is a merely adequate performance from Walken; there have certainly been more memorable villains (and films) in the franchise.

At Close Range (1986) would bring Walken back to somewhere near his best again after a number of films of only reasonable reward. Directed by James Foley, Walken here plays a character old enough to have Sean Penn as his son. It is an under-rated film and Walken, devoid of any saving graces and sporting a truly awful moustache, plays a low rent criminal boss who kills one of his own sons in cold blood. While Penn is overused in the film, the opposite is true of Walken's screen time and the film arguably suffers slightly because of it.

Asked whether the part of his character in the film gave him any insight into his own dark side, Walken has said: "Not really, I think as a matter of fact that I'm so far from it personally, that it's one of the reasons I can do it. I play crazies all the time [but] it sort of rolls off my back. Angst... torture... the twisted things that I play, don't exist that much for me. I have frustration about work, that's about it."[6]

Yet **At Close Range** would mark something of a watershed in terms of Walken's career. Now forty-two years old, the previous years had seen long periods of "resting" between films. With the critical (rather than the meagre commercial) success of the film and his own performance, maybe Walken realised that his age had finally caught up with his face, for he was to work consistently from this point onwards.

In 1988 Walken would get to play alongside Matthew Broderick as a sadistic drillmaster (with emotionally fragile tendencies) in Mike Nichols' **Biloxi Blues**, a bittersweet film based on a Neil Simon play. It was a small but thoroughly memorable role and his chemistry with the much younger cast is palpable.

The sci-fi thriller **Communion** (1989) in retrospect, would be a prototype for what would become the global success of numerous 1990's TV series like *The X-Files* (which would themselves ultimately transmute into feature films). It is less a film about alien abductions as a superficial reading of its themata might imply. More this was a portrait of a madman and Walken playing Whitley Strieber would excel in an otherwise occasionally flawed film.

The first year of the 1990s would find Walken on top form and he would offer up two exceptional performances in a row. First up, **The Comfort Of Strangers** (1990), a brooding, Venice-set thriller, with Walken in particularly creepy mode playing Robert, a Venetian aristocrat with shadowy after dark activities. Helen Mirren, Natasha Richardson and Rupert Everett would also feature and with Dante Spinotte's dense unsettling photography, an intriguingly quirky script by Harold Pinter and assured direction from Paul Schrader (most notable for writing the screenplay for Scorsese's **Taxi Driver**), produced a film that proves both resonant and unsettling.

*The guy I played in **The Comfort Of Strangers**, a man who might possibly exist, I found playing [him] very difficult. He made me very uncomfortable, because to play a person like that you have to somehow get near whatever that is. But whatever connection I made with that guy is something I never dealt with. I just went in front of the camera in a certain mood.*[7]

Later in the year, maverick director Abel Ferrara, responsible for the ultra low-budget and highly controversial **Bad Lieutenant**, with **The King Of New York** (1990), would help coerce Walken into one of the performances of his career (maybe of anyone's career). In this nihilistic and oft-ultra violent thriller, Walken plays Frank White, fresh from the slammer and harbouring dreams of becoming New York's supreme drug dealer. Wesley Snipes, David Caruso and Laurence Fishburne make two cops and a villain respectively in a film that continues to polarise critical and public opinion to the present day.

Influenced heavily by fellow alumni Martin Scorsese and Brian De Palma, Ferrara arguably succeeds in conjoining their individual styles, if only in a darker, rawer version. Yet while there are a few set pieces which are breathtaking, and Ferrara's scary vision of New York (from a script by Nicholas St. John) has an eerie distracted intensity, Walken alone carries the weight of

this film, his quiet intensity a terrifying study of visceral power. Ferrara was to wryly remark during the making of the film, that he was never sure when, or even *if*, Walken was acting.

Yet there was obviously a deep working chemistry between Ferrara and Walken, and they would team up on three further occasions[8]. Come 1995, Walken would be perfectly cast for Ferrara's "vampire" film **The Addiction** playing Peina, proud of his adaptation to eternity. At one point of the film he utters "I'm almost human now..." a quip tailor-made for the actor. A year later would be the often extraordinary film **The Funeral** (1996), with Walken very much part of an ensemble cast in this moody (some critics thought dull) film, a stake-through-the-heart of the Mafia myth. A world away from the glorifying deification of the gangster lifestyle – the speciality of Martin Scorsese and his films **Goodfellas** and **Casino** – **The Funeral**'s realism would share similarities with Mike Newell's acclaimed **Donnie Brasco** which would come out the following year. As in **The King Of New York**, Walken again excels as an underworld crime boss, but here is surrounded by a cast who almost universally provide career-best performances – Annabella Sciorri, Isabella Rosselini and especially Christopher Penn (brother of Sean), who is a revelation.

Between the first two collaborations with Ferrara and after his notable performance in **Batman Returns**, playing a millionaire tycoon ("...He's sort of the Penguin's human agent"), came arguably one of the most celebrated cameo scenes in the Walken canon, in the otherwise disjointed and frenetic Tony Scott directed, Quentin Tarantino written **True Romance** (1993). It is an oft-quoted, infinitely repeatable scene and Walken plays Vincenzo Coccotti, an unhinged Sicilian hood who interrogating Dennis Hopper gets to utter the immortal line "I am the Anti-Christ and you got me in a vendetta kinda mood..." That Walken's frantic intensity manages to steal the thunder from legendary wildman Hopper's best efforts has further helped this sequence achieve almost mythical status.

Dennis Hopper in that scene helped. We helped each other a lot. I always think that actors together is a lot like dancing. You know you dance together. And he was wonderful. He thought I was funny. I thought he was funny. And it shows. I've done two Quentin Tarantino movies and in both cases the dialogue was absolutely written. The words were all there and in **True Romance** *the only thing that's improvised in that scene is [when] he calls me an eggplant and I call him a cantaloupe.*[9]

He would nearly create as memorable a cameo performance the following year playing absolutely deadpan – here as old soldier Captain Coons – in Quentin Tarantino's non-linear and hugely influential ensemble-driven film

Pulp Fiction

Pulp Fiction. A bravura ten-minute monologue done in a single take – a rarity in modern US film-making – of which Walken has said: "It's because I did all those plays. I had to learn big speeches all my life and you kind of get used to talking a lot."[10]

Next up, Walken would play the Angel Gabriel, in Gregory Widen's overlooked religious thriller **Prophecy**. Yet the Angel Gabriel is here a bad angel who scorns the human race as "talking monkeys". Walken has often said that this film and his own performance remains one of his personal favourites.

The year also saw Walken in **Things To Do In Denver When You're Dead**, as a melancholy crime boss (known simply as The Man with the Plan) dispensing threats from his wheelchair in this gallows humour thriller. Though it is a short list, he effortlessly portrays one the most terrifying paraplegics ever committed to celluloid.

With **The Addiction** in the can, he would begin work almost the next

Nick Of Time

day. A critical and commercial failure on it's release, **Nick Of Time** (1995) would star Johnny Depp as a man, forced to murder a State Governor on pain of his daughter's death. Walken as Mr Smith plays the shadowy criminal who plans the deadly event in John Badham's so-so thriller.

His performance as mob henchman Hickey in the Bruce Willis-starring **Last Man Standing** (1996) would be a largely wasted one. Written and directed by Walter Hill, this mutated prohibition era gangster/western would prove an inglorious and dull vanity film for Willis. For Walken, with a dearth of juicy dialogue to chew over and his voice, a deliberately strangled raspy croak, no amount of machine gun fire or snappy sartorial elegance could redeem the performance (or indeed the film as a whole).

With the arrival of 1997, Walken would find himself with his first high profile lead role in years. Starring in **Suicide Kings**, he played Charlie Barret, a former New York Mafia boss who gets captured by rich kids. Walken spends most of the film immobilised (he was tied to a chair), much as he was

in **Denver** a couple of years earlier. It is another fine turn from Walken and though the film did scant business at the box office, it proves that though nearly thirty years had separated him from his first film role to this chronological point, Walken's unique edginess has not deserted him, nor has he resorted to the retro-simulations of earlier film roles. In the last few years Walken has continued to appear in numerous cameo roles and in many cases has proven the highlight of the entire films (and with Walken's legendary intensity, his unbalancing of films was always a problem). He proved he could subtly parody his image and was deadly comical as a mouse exterminator in **Mouse Hunt** (1997), held his own against the combined vocal talents of Gene Hackman, Sylvester Stallone, Sharon Stone and Woody Allen in the much hyped and exceptional digitally animated comedy **Antz** (1998), in a voice-only role as Colonel Cutter. He has also appeared alongside Sissy Spacek, Brendan Fraser and Alicia Silverstone in the nostalgic comedy **Blast From The Past** (1999), as well as the aforementioned **Sleepy Hollow** (1999).

Far removed from the Hollywood lifestyle of self-serving narcissism, networking and scandal-flecked tabloidese, Christopher Walken continues to live in his birthplace New York, in a modest and hardly ostentatious apartment in Manhattans Upper West Side. Both oddly indifferent to the company of others and profoundly reluctant to eat anything he has not cooked himself, Walken rarely goes to parties or restaurants. "There's nothing weird about it. It's common sense. I'm amazed people let total strangers mess around with their food."[11] He collects the occasional painting, rarely ventures out into New York itself and often spends time at his second home, a small farm in Connecticut. He and his wife Georgianna have never had children and Walken to this day, continues to let his films, rather than his private life do the talking.

If you look at my life, it's very conservative, very bourgeois. I'm a foreign actor from another country. I come from the showbiz world and I think it shows. I've been earning money since I was a child and I was always competitive, always looking to see what my position was. And it has an effect on your character. It's a little bit like living in a war zone where you go about your daily life with the shrapnel flying. I don't think that is a natural condition for most people. But I've survived.[12]

NOTES

1. *Sight & Sound* – Jan 1997.

2. *Time Out*, New York.

3. *Empire* – Dec 1997.

4. *Empire* – June 1994.

5. *Empire* – June 1994.

6. *Film Comment* – July/Aug 1992.

7. *Film Comment* – July/Aug 1992.

8. The most recent collaboration between Walken and director Abel Ferrara was **New Rose Hotel** (1998), panned by the critics as confused and risible.

9. www.roughcut.com

10. *The Dark Side*.

11. *The Dark Side*.

12. *Empire* – June 1994.

A BULLET IN THE HEAD: CHRISTOPHER WALKEN IN 'THE DEER HUNTER'

Christopher Walken is Hollywood's angel of death. To paraphrase the man himself in **True Romance**; "You never see evil so singularly personified as in the face of the man who kills you". It's almost as if the line was written for him. No other actor has expressed the pain of mortality so eloquently, so beautifully and so gracefully, whether slayer or slain. From **The Dead Zone** to **The Funeral**, the performances have chronicled death foretold, death administered and death endured; and it is his ravaged, haunted beauty that is at the dark heart of **The Deer Hunter** (1978).

This is a relatively early Walken role, yet there can be little doubt that it is seminal. And of course, it is a performance which spirals inevitably and brilliantly towards death. The film's final third is defined largely by his absence, yet more than the shadowy monologues of **Apocalypse Now**'s Kurtz or the blank countenance of Kubrick's grunts in **Full Metal Jacket**, it is Walken's tortured stare and final, mocking grin that best conveys the desolation of America's spiritual ruin in Vietnam. In remembrance of Walken's deceased character, the closing sequence fuses personal and national loss to a point of incoherence only partly surmountable through a consideration of his performance.

In a huddle of method ticks and introspection, Walken's Nick remains intimate with, yet critical of, Michael (Robert De Niro) and his aspirations to control and (self) mythic transcendence. His accusation that Michael is a "control freak" intensifies his own later loss of control and submission to the myriad seductions of Saigon as it burns and falls. While we first see Nick, Michael and the men of Clairton emerge from the symbolic inferno of a steel mill, it is Nick who opts to remain lost in the sacrificial, redemptive flames of a distant, dying city. The film has been criticized for its dehumanization of the Vietcong but Walken's performance suggests an alternative; the national or spiritual "other" lies not necessarily in the ideological complexities of South East Asia but festers and broods much closer to home.

The film is very much concerned with the construction of American masculinity and this persona is divided chiefly between Michael, with his enigmatic "one shot" ethos and Nick who, initially doubtful of his friend's singular philosophy, ultimately demonstrates the devastating potential of its practice. This is especially ironic given Michael's quest for personal and environmental control, "one shot" finding its purest expression in the familiar ritual of the deer hunt in the mountains. This is intensified by the heavenly

chorus which accompanies Michael's pursuit of his prey. Reticent, aloof and almost introverted, Michael's essential sense of self is demonstrated by the two deer hunting sequences and the possibly internalized choral flourishes of the soundtrack. Nick, on the other hand, paradoxically crystallizes the meaning of "one shot" in a fatal gamble with death, "one shot" as a random, uncontrollable discharge. His descent into the subterranean Russian roulette dens of Saigon epitomizes the film's reduction of its title figure's guiding philosophy, from the affirmative grandeur of the Pennsylvania mountains to a drug-hazed blood sport wherein the gun is pointed only at oneself. Just as Michael's drive for control reflects the nation's own sense of imperial authority then Nick's (not entirely unconscious) rejection of his homeland represents its collective, psychic collapse. If Michael's quasi-mythic persona reveals that to which America aspires, Nick's physical and mental disintegration demonstrate truly what it has become.

Nevertheless, the film emphasises their love amidst the mounting layers of social and psychological collapse. The men of **The Deer Hunter** are some of the least articulate you are ever likely to encounter on the screen and thus, the essence of their relationships lies often in what remains half uttered or even unsaid. The film's complex interconnections of ritual and ceremony bind the male characters both physically and spiritually, and Nick's oft-times mediating presence is a crucial structural element. His are the first audible words of the film, an appalling joke about cunnilingus ("Did you hear about the happy Roman? He was glad he ate her!") as the men bathe in the exhilaration of a completed workday. Yet, amid the swirl of macho-sexist bravado, he sights the vain preening of Stan (the late, great John Cazale) and tells him mockingly, "it's no use". As the group leave the mill, Nick's elegant swagger sets him apart from the other men, his posture and manner hinting at an otherwise unexpressed sexual poise.

This is complemented by the ensuing sequence in the bar in which Walken croons and shakes a hip to the strains of "I Love You Baby" during a homoerotically charged game of pool. Indeed, one might venture that his character is almost "feminized" (if one accepts grace and poise as predominantly "feminine" characteristics) in a ruck of repressive hyper masculinity. That the men should join in a raucous chorus of the song only serves to underline Nick's incongruous elegance amongst the crowd. "I like a man with good moves and speed" is how Michael later defines his preference for Nick over the other "assholes" he calls his friends. It is a characteristic that Nick demonstrates with aplomb during the film's extended wedding sequence. Walken's experience as a dancer is utilized forcefully to convey Nick's relative integration into the structures of the community and during the wedding, in his capacity as best man, he becomes the undoubted focus of the men's potential for social expressions of joy and exuberance.

Michael Cimino's handling of this sequence is a startling integration of intimacy and spectacle, locating Walken centrally in both the disruptive and harmonious undercurrents of family and community.

Yet, male intimacy on a one to one basis is suddenly marked by fractured, enigmatic expressions; "I like the trees... the way the trees are" sighs Nick before he, Steven (John Savage) and Michael set off on the 24 hours comprising the wedding, their final hunt and their journey to fight a distant war. Striving in vain to voice his own sense of the poetic quality of the surrounding landscape, Nick cuts himself off self-consciously, fearful that his insight makes him "sound like some asshole". After a drunken, post-wedding streak, Nick maintains Michael's dignity by covering his nakedness before exhorting him to not "leave me over there". These malformed exclamations of fear, love and intimacy dictate the final movement of the film wherein the implicit love of the two men finds expression only through Michael's desperate quest to fulfil Nick's plea.

Nick and Michael share a home together, a small prefabricated shack which stands beneath the ominous shadow of the mill in which they work. While alluding to the established historical and literary mythology of the log cabin, the two men represent a split in the individual ethos of the traditionally constructed American male. Consequently, the film's oscillation between Michael and Nick highlights both the external threat and internal tensions of the central male couple. Nick repeatedly expresses his views of Michael's self containment; "Are you trying to look like a prince?", he ribs his friend before the wedding, recalling his earlier taunting of Stan, while soon afterwards simply calling him a "fucking nut". Yet for all of his insight into Michael's peculiar vanities, Nick remains faithful to him. Stan, whose own sexual insecurities are manifested through misogyny and homophobia, repeatedly accuses Michael of being a "faggot" or of spouting "faggot sounding bullshit". Brandishing a single bullet amidst the splendour of the Pennsylvania mountains, Michael's contemptuous and enigmatic proclamation to Stan that "this is this" at once expresses his belief in "one shot" while hinting at a singular purity of existence. After Michael's almost childish refusal to loan Stan a pair of boots during the hunt, it is Nick who intervenes, scolding him with a disbelieving "What's the matter with you?". Nick's mounting rejection of Michael's ideals coupled with the horrific experience and aftermath of the war, demonstrate that "this" is most certainly not simply "this" any more.

The prevalent but fearful yearning for male intimacy influences Nick's own sense of judgement. The extent to which this affects his romantic involvement with Linda (Meryl Streep) is crucial, infusing their relationship with an array of disruptions. During their first sequence together, Michael views their intimate exchange from within the shack the two men occupy. Framed precisely within the confines of a window, Michael's point of view of the couple suggests the inexorable binds of the masculine relationship and how Nick's affair with Linda is shaped by, and serves to threaten, the primacy of the male relationship. Appropriately, the wedding sequence, while formally entranced by the intricate ceremony of matrimony, demonstrates the multiple socio-sexual tensions which infiltrate at every level. Furthermore, it exemplifies the paradox of the customs and beliefs of old world communities as they are absorbed into the melting pot of the United States. For the men of Clairton, their bonding rituals bear only nominal traces of the religious or ethnic foundations of the town and the wedding becomes as much a "celebration" of Nick, Michael and Steven's imminent service in Vietnam as it is of the holy binds of marriage itself. Indeed, the hall in which the party takes place is adorned with giant high school images of Nick and Michael as if in acknowledgement of their own "marriage". These flank an image of Steven, anticipating their guardianship and protection of him in Vietnam.

Nick serves as Steven's best man at the wedding, a role which emphasizes both his proximity to the groom and his position within the community at large. He and Linda represent the community's "golden couple", their function as best man and chief bridesmaid a precursor to their own marriage. Therefore, Michael's furtive glances and clumsy attempts to charm Linda is as much an attempt to halt the loss of Nick to another lover than to fulfil his own desire for her. This dynamic is complemented by Nick's insistence that Linda dance with Michael, whose inept social skills preclude the same level of integration achieved by Nick. Perhaps tacitly recognizing Michael's attraction to Linda, Nick offers her to his male "partner" in deference to their own repressed bond.

Yet, the wedding also affords Walken's Nick the opportunity to further demonstrate the subtle contrasts he represents to De Niro's Michael. As if in another gentle mocking of the "one shot" enigma, he performs a jokey ritual in which a beer glass is hurdled after the third attempt. This short vignette enlists the symbol of the beer glass as a complement to the gun, a strategy which is continued throughout the film in order to define the bonding rituals of the male group. Moreover, Nick's "offering" of Linda to Michael is followed by a brief but poignant shot in which he observes their flight from the dance floor in a silent, passive glance as he chivalrously holds the floor with an ugly duckling. Contained within that classic Walken look (the trace of a nod, the faint smile that seems to twist into a grimace) is the unspoken foreknowledge of imminent traumas, unfulfilled destinies. It is from that moment perhaps that realization dawns that *he*, at least, will never be coming back. Nick's earlier demonstrations of tenderness and understanding with Linda, her face marked by her father's assault, are countered by Michael's awkward offers to Linda to buy her a beer. Whereas such awkwardness and violence (for example, Stan's punching of his girlfriend on the dancefloor after the master of ceremonies strokes her behind) seem endemic amongst the men, Nick's sensitivity once more marks his separation from the homosocial strictures of the community.

This isn't to suggest that Nick, before the traumatic realizations of Vietnam, seeks to transcend or even escape the limits of Clairton. "I love this fuckin' town" he exclaims to Michael before his plea to never leave him in Vietnam. As Michael's partner, he is at the forefront of each mode of masculine activity be it work, the hunt or the war, but at each stage he is the provider of mediating levels of insight and action. Accordingly, he is prominent in the wedding celebrations while Michael conceals himself at the peripheries of the room. In a misguided, drunken high, Nick attempts to ingratiate a green beret on leave from the war who has somehow infiltrated the wedding celebrations. "I hope they send us where the bullets are flying and the fighting is the worst," he blurts, only to be met with a contemptuous, almost demonic riposte of "fuck it". Of course, Nick's own eventual descent into near catatonia perversely fulfils his ill-considered wish. The outward rejection of fear belies the men's silent dread of the impending trip to Vietnam and it is Nick who becomes the resonant personification of that fear. Before the hunting trip, Nick is asked by one of the men, "how come I never see you eat?". His seemingly flippant reply is "I like to starve myself, it keeps the fear up". Once more, this fleeting allusion to a deeper yet enigmatic personal philosophy aligns him with Michael while emphasizing his fundamental differences. The notion of "fear" is alien to Michael's drive to control and self-assertion but it infuses Nick with almost prophetic insight. His fear is given shape, definition and ultimately, meaning through his experiences in both the jungle and urban landscapes of Vietnam.

Occurring in the aftermath of the 1968 Tet offensive, the film presents, in some respects, a war already lost. The striking narrative ellipses are particularly pronounced in the Vietnam sequence, yet their jarring effect conveys forcefully the rapid erosion of the ideals established tentatively in the film's first hour. The "one shot" philosophy is immediately questioned by Michael's incineration and machine gunning of an enemy soldier and the ceremony and ritual of the wedding and deer hunt find their terrible complement in the jungle warfare and games of enforced Russian roulette with the Vietcong. In Vietnam, the rituals of human interaction are marked by the film's reduction of men to objects of exchange. The veracity of the Russian roulette sequence has been much questioned but Cimino's stated intention of it as metaphor buttresses the film's examination of human capital value as it is defined by cultures at war. The Clairton steel mill serves to define the men's class position within their own culture. However, as tools of imperialist intervention, their social position is crystallized by their status as bargaining chips by the enemy in a deadly gamble with fate.

The Russian roulette game places Nick and Steven at the mercy of not only their Vietcong captors but also that of Michael. In another rejection of "one shot", Michael decides that the only chance of escape lies in the attempt to play the game with *more* bullets. Yet Michael's decision to forget about Steven, increasingly traumatized by his ordeal, is met with Nick's riposte, "Who do you think you are, God?". Nick's criticism of Michael's decision also rejects the self-deification implicit in the choral accompaniment to the deer hunt. The visual construction of the male group (defined as family) which adorns the walls of the wedding celebration is ironically consolidated here, in the face of its very annihilation. Michael's patriarchal role is marked by his defiance and aggression in the face of his captors. He is the architect of the escape while both Nick and Steven are, respectively, feminized and infantilized by their weeping and hysteria.

Caged and submerged in water, Walken initially expresses Nick's anguish through a series of silent glares. Almost in anticipation of his own imminent fate, he stares wide-eyed yet blankly at a cadaverous (but still living) American prisoner suspended and eerily sedate in the water. That smile-cum-grimace is utilized to full effect during the game, disbelieving laughter transforming into distressed tears as the gun's hammer clicks without discharge against his head. The Russian roulette game epitomizes the split between Nick and Michael, their enforced playing against each other manifesting the latent but always apparent ruptures in their relationship. Indeed, the homoerotic dimension adopts a distinctly sadistic dimension, affirming Michael's drive to control and domination. Michael's "more bullets" gamble physically saves the men from their captors but leads to the final breakdown of their social and communal bond. The ideological confusions and ambiguities of the war are exemplified (at least for the Americans) by the grotesque intimacy of the Russian roulette sequence and the film progresses to express the impossibility of moral reconstruction in its aftermath.

Nick's isolation and estrangement in Saigon intensifies the sense of his (and, of course, Walken's) associations with mortality. During his stay in the hospital, he is depicted reclining in a window frame overlooking rows of khaki-draped corpses which litter the lawn beneath a faintly fluttering stars and stripes flag. Retreating into confusion, his entire concept of self, family, community and nation are neutralized. Upon questioning from an officer he insists that his Russian surname is "American" yet further interrogation reveals that he cannot remember his parents' birthdays. He stares intently at a photograph of Linda but abandons his attempt to call her on a telephone. Upon meeting a prostitute, he calls her "Linda" but flees her room upon sighting her child. The underlying familial, sexual, masculine and communal tensions in Clairton are given full expression in Saigon. Relationships are marked outwardly as exploitative through their place within a diseased, corrupted value system defined principally through prostitution and gambling. Unwilling to fully negotiate the socio-political structures of Clairton, the film transplants the American town's underlying tensions onto the depiction of Saigon and Nick becomes the potent human manifestation of the diseased, dying city. The contaminatory nature of the war is literalized by the gangrene-infested wounds of Steven yet it is Nick's refusal to return to Clairton that stops the infection from being completely terminal. Nick is introduced to organized Russian roulette by a sketchily defined, almost spectral Frenchman. These two colonial phantoms complement the sense that Saigon has become a site for capitalism reduced to its basest level. Unaware of Michael's presence in the room, Nick seizes the stage and contemptuously pulls the trigger. In his final rejection of the monetary inflections of the "game", he hurls his cash winnings away from a car as the unseen Michael pursues him in desperation and hordes of street dwellers scramble for the discarded currency.

To what extent Nick "remembers" home becomes clouded and obscure. Michael's visit to Steven (who like Nick, his surrogate "mother" figure, refuses to return to Clairton) in a war veteran's centre reveals that Nick has been sending thousands of dollars through the mail, presumably money acquired through his participation in organized Russian roulette. The fruits of corrupt capitalism are channelled back to the USA in the form of benign benefaction and rather than maintaining any form of link with Michael or Linda, Nick maintains an indirect communication with Steven, now physically disabled through the loss of his legs. The implicit rejection of Michael and Linda (and their inter-related functions of partner/lover) is aligned with the links maintained with Steven, whose physical deterioration mirrors Nick's mental state. The tangible consequences of the war are defined through physical and psychological breakdown and their resultant disruption of familial and community ties. Michael's return to Clairton cannot repair this, his presence only serving to intensify the ambience of despair and loss. He has lost his crucial link to the male group, he rejects the communal welcoming party and finds solace only in Linda, the closest connection to his absent companion. Nick's absence from Clairton represents a perverse transcendence of both self and community, a state to which Michael has aspired yet manifestly failed to achieve. Michael's return to Clairton only confirm the unattainability of his "one shot" ideal while Nick's breakdown in Saigon hints at an attainment of self-realization achievable only through physical, psychological and spiritual collapse.

The ultimate revelation of Nick's drug addiction completes the perceived cycle of vice in Saigon (prostitution, gambling, narcotics). Yet the final reconciliation of Nick and Michael portrays the former as unaware of the latter's identity, shedding his friend's previous influence in a chemically alleviated trauma. Michael's search for Nick leads him back into the symbolic fire whence they emerged at the beginning of the film, represented this time by the dying embers of the Saigon streets. Nick's earlier function within both the community and the male group, stressing his sensitivity, warmth and extrovert qualities, has been decimated. His primary function now is as an object of corrupt exchange. The ceremonial aspect of the organized Russian roulette game is stressed by the red headband that the players tie around their heads yet it is ritual dictated not by quasi-spiritual or philosophical forces (as with the deer hunt and its one shot associations) but by money. Nick's inability (or refusal) to recognize Michael is articulated not only verbally but through a defiant gob of spit to Michael's face. This is a brutally jarring moment, not only for Michael's passive lack of retaliation but for the glazed relish with which Nick briefly surveys his deed up close. It is the closest the men come to face to face intimacy throughout the film, the male romance at once confirmed by their physical proximity but denied by Nick's contemptuous action.

In fulfilling Nick's wish that he should not leave him in Vietnam, Michael merely discovers the irreparable break between them. The brief prelude to Nick's final "game" amplifies his rejection of Michael's philosophy ("one shot" reduced to a single, ball of spittle) while bringing them to their most candid exchange of emotions. Feelings previously left unsaid are suddenly articulated amidst the intensity of baying men and wagered money. Michael's admission, "I love you Nick", is accompanied by his references to the issues they discussed back home in the sanctuary of their shared home. Michael's attempt to make Nick "remember the trees" refers to the latter's earlier, half-expressed appreciation of their surroundings yet it is a detail precious to both men and their bond of intimacy. Nick's enigmatic half gestures and seeming near-recollections make Michael's pleading all the more hollow. In a final moment of clarity, a sudden recollection of "one shot" and a grimly laconic "yeah!", Nick at once accepts and denies the declaration of love, seemingly confirming recognition but obliterating it with a single bullet to the head. As Nick's wound spurts furiously, his face is transformed into a grotesquely peaceful death mask, his mouth gaping open as his blood weeps through the sobbing Michael's desperately caressing hands. Blood and tears flow in unison as the film's death and love motifs conjoin bitterly and tragically. For Nick, this bullet marks his final, inevitable submission to the vagaries of chance, a moment perversely but tellingly retained for his reconciliation with Michael. Yet, paradoxically it is one shot as the culmination of many, the terminal gesture in an extended flirtation with death.

Echoing the earlier window image of Nick and Linda, the film's closing moments briefly frame Michael from within the dark interior of a hearse but this time emphasizing the mortal separation from Nick. Peering sombrely through the back windshield which physically detaches him from his deceased friend, Michael is left to ponder the unfulfilled declaration of love as a choir once more swells on the soundtrack. If the funeral wake's final rendition of "God Bless America" remains loaded with ambiguity, the affinity and affection for Nick is resolutely affirmed. This final expression of personal and national mourning seems to endorse Nick's status as communal figurehead while lamenting the ideals which his passing has been instrumental in obliterating. Despite its structural and thematic richness (or perhaps because of it) the film is torn between its final toast to the departed and the patriotic impulses such a devastated community would appear to negate. Amid the slow agonies of war and the crumbling ideals of individual, community and nation, it is Nick's decisive "one shot" that truly brings it all back home.

'BRAINSTORM'

Even searching on the internet, the world wide web that is library of all from
Manimal to The Plastic Jesus Song, you won't find much about the film
Brainstorm (1983). If not a forgotten film, it is certainly not a well-
remembered one. A few anaemic reviews of the Leonard Maltin ilk, the odd
bit of trivia (for example, did you know that the Brainstorm headsets were re-
used in **Spacehunter: Adventures In The Forbidden Zone**, a dumb but
enter-taining science fiction flick which appeared during the second burst of
3-D movies?), and that's pretty much it. Even Walken interviews are more
likely to mention Mickey Rourke's slugfest **Homeboy** than they are
Brainstorm. The problem with **Brainstorm** is that it is only really known for
one thing; not the special effects, technical innovations or performances, but
the fact that it was Natalie Wood's final film. All other details seem to be
obscured because Natalie Wood drowned before the film's completion, after
falling off a boat moored a mere fifty foot from shore. From that point on,
hack journalists could start mustering conspiracy theories. The attempted air
of mystery and press angle of the time was that Wood's husband, Robert
Wagner, had been fighting with Walken after discovering he was having an
affair with her. After all the theorising, the simple fact is that Natalie Wood,
who was unable to swim, slid on a slippery deck and drowned.

Walken was frequently asked about this incident (and very seldom
about the film itself) but kept a tactful silence until interviewed by *Playboy* in
September, 1997. Walken is plainly annoyed by the handling of the incident,
especially by the coroner, Thomas Noguchi (Walken: "Wasn't that guy kicked
out as chief medical examiner for being an asshole?"). With the sad death of
Natalie Wood, the film's fate seemed pretty much sealed. Though principal
photography was almost completed, the studio was more interested in
scrapping the project and collecting the insurance than seeing the film reach
the cinemas. Fortunately director Doug Trumbull's contract gave him final say
in this situation and he managed to soldier on through all this adversity,
forcing the studio to allow him to complete the picture using a stand-in for
Wood's final scenes. **Brainstorm** was eventually released in 1983 to middling
reviews and poor box office receipts.

Brainstorm is far from faultless, but it does throw up some
interesting ideas, has some intriguing special effects (especially for the early
eighties) and has two knockout central performances.

Brainstorm is very much a film of the early eighties when computer
technology was first influencing the Hollywood film community (see also the
Disney computer graphic extravaganza **Tron**). Doug Trumbull was certainly
the director for the job, having previously directed eco-robot yarn **Silent
Running** and being the special effects maestro for **Close Encounters Of The**

Third Kind and **2001**. The film's main flaws are a narrative which suffers from cliché and confusion, and the burst of ridiculous robot comedy, which sits uneasily with the philosophical elements of the tale. Thematically it is now viewed as an important precursor to Katherine Bigelow's techno nightmare **Strange Days**, which takes the basic premise of **Brainstorm** (a person's extreme sensory experiences can be recorded and played back in another's minds to either stimulating or devastating effect) and throws it into the arena of hyper-paced detective thriller.

But **Brainstorm** was not the first film to deal with such subject matter; for this, one has to journey back to the world of the British "B" horror movie. Before Louise Fletcher and Christopher Walken started dabbling in taping mind experience, Boris Karloff and Catherine Lacey had paved the way – albeit in a more primitive fashion – in **The Sorcerors**.

The Sorcerors was a small British movie made by Michael Reeves, cult director of **Witchfinder General** and tragically youthful suicide victim. In the story Boris Karloff and Catherine Lacey are an old couple who, through hypnosis and technology, discover a way to relive the sensations of youth via the experiences of tearaway (and Saint to be) Ian Ogilvy. Commencing with the simple pleasure of a moonlight swim, the old woman becomes increasingly addicted to extremes of robbery, murder and fast driving. Finally, Ogilvy crashes his car and in the ensuing fireball is burnt to death, an experience which also destroys our aging scientists. Though crude by the standards of **Brainstorm**, **The Sorcerors** deals in the basics of taking the physical experiences of one person to be played through another's mind and, like **Brainstorm**, starts with our scientists sampling the simple pleasures and then becoming increasingly obsessive about the deeper recesses of the mind.

From the dazzlingly colourful opening credits of **Brainstorm** one can see that director Trumbull is on a mission to impress. Firstly the titles and credits curve outwards into the audience in almost 3-D fashion, then we see a series of three dimensional shapes and patterns which we find out are test cards being transmitted to the mind of Michael Brace (Christopher Walken) via a sensory headset. We are in the scientists' lair where Michael and Lilian Reynolds (Louise Fletcher, chain smoking throughout as all cynics in movies have to do) are on the point of completing Brainstorm, a system to transfer sensory experiences of one mind to another, with the assistance of Jenkins (Alan Fudge) and Gordy (Jordan Christopher). Brace experiences everything Gordy does, from a literal knee jerk reaction to the taste sensation of steak and marshmallow with a cherry on top, the noise of a synthesizer that wouldn't look out of place in Rick Wakeman's attic and finishing with the distress of a laboratory monkey (a lab assistant practical joke). After a moment of fear that the monkey joke has addled his brain, Brace rises from his chair and declares the headset an unqualified success, and the team toast their triumph with a can of beer shared out between four glass beakers.

Michael returns home, where his marriage to Karen (Natalie Wood) has disintegrated due to his scientific obsession, and toasts a picture of Einstein in his den. Head of the company, Alex Terson (Cliff Robertson) wants to go straight into production of Brainstorm, with Karen co-ordinating design, Lilian approaches this with a cynical air. The team go into a hefty recording schedule with the ebullient, lecherous Gordy experiencing everything from water slides to Grand Prix racing. The military are soon sniffing around and, at a celebratory party, Michael and Lilian discover the depth of army interest. They are forced to work with scientist, and fed spy, Landon Marks, loathed by Lilian for his hackery. Lilian storms off, infuriated by Michael's naivety and Alex's selling out of the project (however unwillingly), and suffers terrible chest pains (from the first stabbing chest pain we can be pretty sure we will not be seeing Lilian at the end of the movie). The military's reason is of course, the protection of the American people, when in truth they have seen the headset's obvious applications in everything from missile guidance to brainwashing. Other scientists, such as Gordy, have seen the potential for the hardest-core pornography, while Michael turns to it as a RELATE councillor, discovering through replayed memories where his marriage went wrong. Replaying memories of their past, Michael's marriage is repaired, but then he receives a call from Jenkins, wife. Jenkins has taken a small amount of tape from the "porn showreel" and is stuck in coital convulsions. Feeling better than he has felt in years, Jenkins decides to take indefinite paid leave, but still suffers twitching flashbacks.

Meanwhile, Lilian is working in the lab when she suffers chest pains; dying from a heart attack, she places the Brainstorm headset on to record the brain's final experiences before death. After the funeral, Michael attempts to experience Lilian's tape but is gripped by vicious heart pains, while Landon Marks and the military look on with Gordy (now on the side of the Feds) also wired up. Gordy cannot take the pain, and is killed. Michael, though, has disconnected the heart and respiratory sensors of Brainstorm and travels through Lilian's dying memories (their early experiments in robotics, surprise birthday parties and battles with Alex), before a worried Jenkins disconnects him.

After a period of recovery, Michael makes a pact with Karen that he must view Lilian's tape. Upon returning to the laboratory, Michael discovers that Landon Marks and has taken over the project and therefore he is effectively locked out; though furious, Michael seems secure in the knowledge that they will be unable to decipher his notes.

The headsets are now in mass production. Michael hacks into the computer (codename: Brainstorm) and finds that the program will be used for brainwashing and neurological tortures of all kinds. Appalled, he downloads

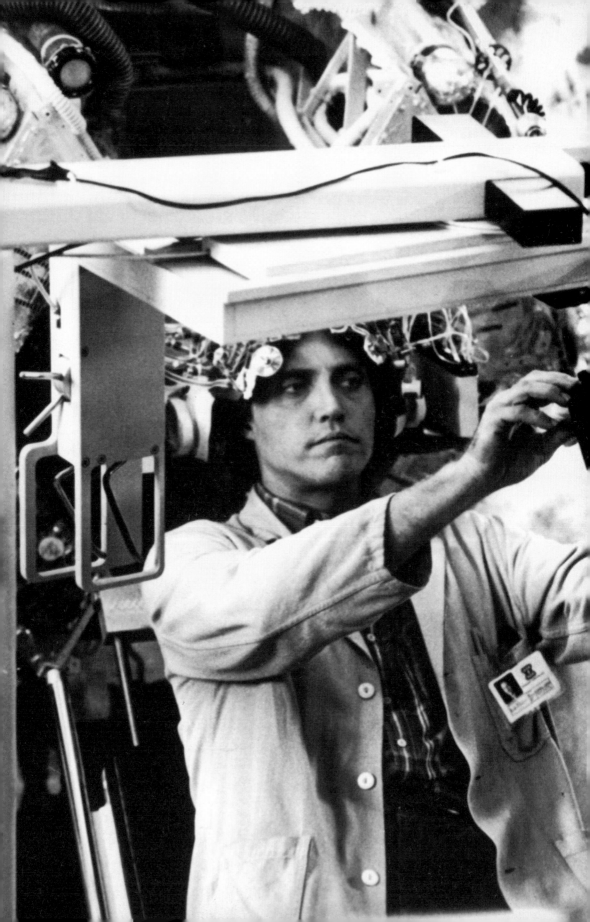

a tape but is unable to stand its intensity. While explaining to Karen how Alex has sold them out, his son experiences the tape and is thrown into a nightmarish world of his worst fears (being attacked and experimented on by Michael) and is hospitalised.

Michael and Karen agree to take a break, though they know they are being tailed by military spies. Using the pretence of a public row, Karen storms off, in fact going to Jenkins' house where she will tap into the Brainstorm computer, while Michael utilises a hotel phone to gain access to Lilian's tape.

The laboratory is sabotaged and in the ensuing mayhem Michael accesses the tape. Michael goes off to the place where he first experienced a love of science and courted Karen – Kill Devil Hill, the national park where the Wright Brothers experimented with flight. First seeing Lilian's struggling organs, he then journeys to Heaven and a host of angels. Karen fears that the experience has killed him, but he awakes, astonished and overjoyed at his vision. The government has been beaten, his marriage has been restored and he has glimpsed Heaven.

Some opinion says that **Brainstorm** is dazzlingly original, but the plot falls into cliché a few times too often: from the hard-knuckled maverick, chain smoking and bullish, whose death midway spurs on our hero; the evil eye of the military (white haired and bug-eyed) ready to destroy all the good in the scientists' discovery; the crumbling marriage which always accompanies those of vision; to the happy ending which takes us into Capraesque realms. The plot lacks a darkness which would have made it all the more compelling; if you imagine it under the tutelage of someone like David Cronenberg, you can see the potential for a truly chilling film. This is not director Doug Trumbull's fault, but more that of storywriter Bruce Joel Rubin. Rubin has continued to show his obsession with death in his work since **Brainstorm** with a romantic thriller, a horror thriller and a drama, but his death obsession is ultimately rose-tinted. The romantic tearjerker **Ghost** was an enormous hit and won Rubin an Academy Award for best screenplay, while **Jacob's Ladder**, starring Tim Robbins, appeared to be a far darker look at a man suffering bizarre flashbacks and hallucinations (or are they real?) after being given experimental drugs in Vietnam (eventually we discover that all his life post-Vietnam has been a fiction, as he died during the war). The majority of the latter film is quite entertaining, with some very spooky images, but the ending is a terrible cop out, with Robbins' dead son (Macauley Culkin) leading him up some stairs to Heaven. Were the previous two hours a man being judged if he should go to Heaven or just flickerings through a dying mind? Anyone who watches this movie will be far more satisfied if they turn off before the final five minutes. Rubin's final exploration of death was with Michael Keaton in **My Life**, with Keaton videotaping his life for his unborn

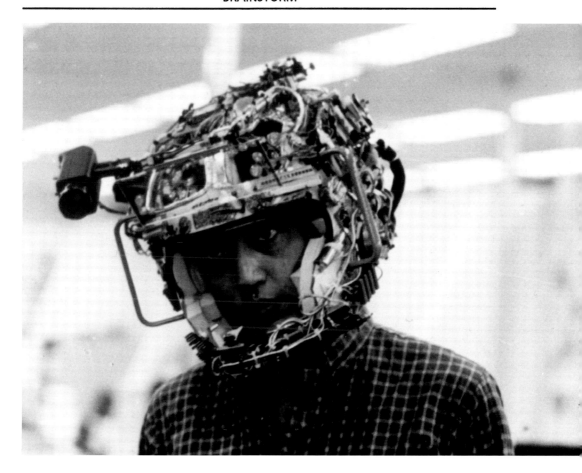

child to view after his death. The less said the better. **Brainstorm** seems to be the story that can stand the most further viewing (unless you're a clay-loving couple who have only recently started dating, then obviously turn to **Ghost**).

The two central performances of **Brainstorm** are magnificent. Louise Fletcher dominates the first half of the film as Lilian. She portrays the intensity of a driven scientist, determined to succeed and full of self-belief. She has clearly sacrificed everything else in her life to create what many would see as the impossible. Yet her chain smoking, even though she knows she has a heart condition, betrays the self-destructing nature of the genius. So close to achieving her life's ambition, is she ready to die? Even in her death throes she still has to give herself to science. She also perfectly embodies the cynicism of someone who knows they'll be fucked over. The moment she sees the military she knows she is going to be done again, but that doesn't stop her fighting to keep her creation from the hacks she despises. Fletcher's standout scene is undoubtedly when Landon Marks is thrust upon the project ("Don't take my project. This is my project and I don't want to see it on some defence scrapheap before we know what it's capable of"); the pain, rage and emotion of this scene give an intensity to the film unusual for much science fiction. The sensory headset is her child, she does not guard it because she is jealous of others' involvement, but because she knows that others will taint it. When the super-conducting chip they need to make the headset marketable is revealed by Alex, Fletcher perfectly conveys both Lilian's happiness and her fear that her invention shall soon be wrenched from her laboratory where she can protect "her offspring" from the world. The relationship between Lilian and Michael also has a great amount of charm, never romantic, but more a love affair of science. What seems so surprising watching Fletcher is that, despite performances such as this and **One Flew Over The Cuckoo's Nest**, she has been stuck in such tat for the rest of her career (anyone for **Firestarter** or **Best Of The Best**?).

Christopher Walken is pretty much incapable of turning in an uninteresting performance. However poor the material, Walken can drag something interesting out of it (even the tedious and fortunately forgotten **War Zone**). Pauline Kael once said that Bill Murray was one of the only good reasons to visit the cinema, and the same could be said of Walken. Walken in 1981 wasn't the eccentric fixture of the screen that we think of now, though he had been brilliantly effective in **The Deer Hunter** and **Annie Hall** and had a chance to show off the dancing abilities of his youth in **Pennies From Heaven**. Walken had also played Stanley Kowalski for laughs in a stage version of "A Streetcar Named Desire" to avoid being compared to Brando ("It was a stitch, but a lot of people criticised me for doing that. But what the fuck was I supposed to do?"). This is the kind of bizarre decision that marks out Walken as such a vibrant performer – however motionless he appears. When required he always manages to bring both an other-worldliness *and* humanity to his performances.

His work in the eighties is tremendously wide ranging, embracing thrillers, family dramas, musicals, comedy (his brilliant turn in **Biloxi Blues**) and even a Bond movie. By the end of the eighties, Walken would be a target of US comedy impressionists; at the beginning, he was not quite so quantifiable. Walken's alien countenance is used to fine and unsettling effect whenever he plays those outside the mainstream and Michael is another of those personalities, though certainly saner than most of Walken's screen characters. Michael is a character who evolves through self-discovery provided by his own creation; through his own obsessive scientific quest he rediscovers himself. Walken's face always seem so glacial that the registering of any emotion, even the slightest facial twitch, seem to convey so much more than with the majority of actors. In the opening scene, his eyes have such intensity about them, not only is he conveying that he is not in this world (he is experiencing Gordy's senses), but the immense importance of this experiment; the intensity of his endeavour. Walken's comic ability is often underrated, as anyone who has seen his turns on "Saturday Night Live" will know, but his snarl when all around him think he may have been affected by being plugged into a monkey's brain, is akin to his brief dance when he has what appears to be having a stand-off at the beginning of **King Of New York**, a triumphant breaking of cinematic tension. Walken has sometimes been described as scary (a term he doesn't like, he says he would rather be considered spooky, "after all a horse can be spooked"), and his delivery of lines can indeed have a spooky air. When he sees Karen with her new love at the celebration party for the headset's success, his delivery of "You look nice" has an air of menace, confusion and annoyance that he cannot really work out where he has gone wrong in the relationship. His lack of understanding in his mishandling of his marriage is a key to his character; he has desire, but how can he express it? He cannot understand how Karen can have misconstrued his clumsy and arrogant handling of this relationship. This is further emphasised when he experiences Karen's unfettered thoughts through the headset. As Walken replays his memories, we see how his ambition has blotted everything else in his life. His initial anger at seeing Karen's true emotion ("that's not me you're seeing"), and Lilian's understanding of the both of them (even though she has given up everything to pursue her scientific desire) is a key point in a confused plot. Walken's outburst, both directed at Karen and himself, is a great Walken flip-out moment.

Walken's experiences are there to show us the possible good of the creation, though his return to harmony seems all to easy; if only they'd just bothered to remember the good old days in the first place. Natalie Wood is stuck with a thankless part. We learn little of her. She exists purely as a cipher to show us the ultimate good within Michael. She is there to help him, love him and understand him; as a final role it offers few rewards. She might be a great designer, but ultimately she is a wife and a mother. Walken's naive handling of his relationship is also reflected in his initial reactions to the rapid development of the headset. His youthful immersion in science has obviously not readied him for the fight ahead. Like the twentieth century nuclear scientist, he cannot comprehend that anyone would wish to use his creation for ill. Once the battle commences we see a new Michael, a Michael who has made the journey from the antiseptic laboratory to the dirty outside world and beaten it, for the time being at least.

In many ways, Michael is one of Walken's most straight-forward roles, and one of his few as the hero. Without Walken's presence I believe this would be a far less watchable film, his bizarre qualities as an actor make

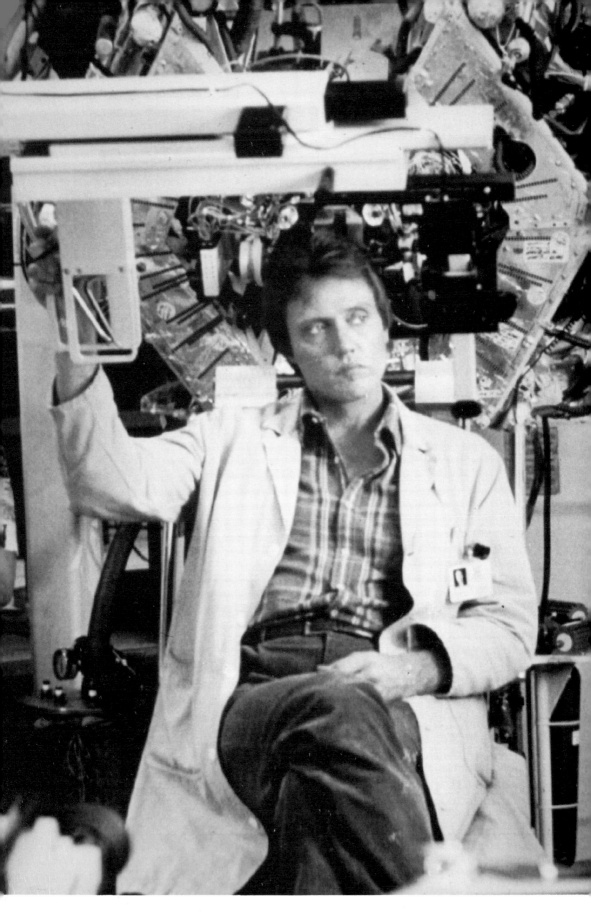

Michael a fascinating cinematic scientist. Yet despite the depth he can bring to seemingly normal personalities, Walken's opinion of acting is not what one might expect from a New York actor. In interviews he seems to view his acting as strangely artless, believing he doesn't the ability others have. "I don't have a process... I see actors who really transform themselves, I don't think I do that. I don't really care if I'm an actor or not. I do care about being able to do it in order to make a good living."

For Walken it comes down to being able to work. "I was a dancer once and I had a T shirt that said 'Shut Up And Dance', and acting gets like that." For a man that brings so much to every film he appears in, however small the part, and who has become such a cult phenomenon, he has a fascinatingly bullshitless approach. He is aware of his strange aura and sees it merely as a way to be in work. Fortunately for us, the work indeed seems to keep coming in.

For a director from a special effects background, Doug Trumbull manages to make a film that avoids overt gloss and too much dazzling of the senses. He deals with the scenes between Michael and Karen with a sensitivity and maturity again unusual in the genre. (His previous directed film was **Silent Running**, another mature piece of science fiction with an ecology bent that also had an otherworldly leading man in the shape of Bruce Dern.) Unfortunately, his masterstroke in the film is unlikely to be viewed properly now. Trumbull uses 35mm and 70mm in **Brainstorm**, with 70mm being used for the sensory playback sequences – an enticing innovation.

The likelihood now is that you'll be viewing it on the small screen, which for a film that wishes to astound you with its visuals, is highly disappointing. The journey to Heaven still has some nice touches, though special effects have moved on at such a pace that some may be left underwhelmed. The chorus of angels of light may be magnificent on the big screen but seem a little hokey and unimaginative on the television. Perhaps on DVD and a widescreen TV you may go some of the way to recreating the effect, but it takes a leap of imagination to realise how cinematically effective this was at the time. Since **Brainstorm**, Trumbull has not directed another cinema feature, which seems a pity as both his entries in the science fiction genre have been quirky and interesting, if not wholly successful. Trumbull now creates sensurround films for theme parks in Japan – a natural progression, perhaps, from **Brainstorm**.

The trouble with **Brainstorm** is really in the pacing of the plot. It could happily be two films; a science fiction conspiracy thriller or a science fiction love story. The film takes too long to become a thriller and the love story doesn't dominate enough for that to solely work either. Too many moments seem to exist as if plot points put in by someone who has just read a copy of "How To Write A Screenplay In Three Easy Stages". Michael's son need hardly exist at all and his induced nightmare vision is distinctly lacklustre. The trashing of the factory by the robots is also a piece of light relief thrown in far too late to be effective and sitting awkwardly with the tension built up around Michael's attempt to view Lilian's tape. Ninety minutes into a reasonably humourless film is way too late to have security guards slipping over ballbearings, being immersed in soap suds and other such Keystone mayhem. Having one of the robots appear to laugh is also a strange addition to an already overdone scene. Lilian and Michael also seem to be the only two characters who are properly drawn.

Ultimately, **Brainstorm** fits in that awkward category of adult science fiction where films such as Mike Hodges' **The Terminal Man**, Donald Cammell's **Demon Seed** and Trumbull's own **Silent Running** also reside. These are the kind of non-formula films that modern Hollywood would now be wary of making, but they make up an interesting sub-genre in their attempts to deal with ideas beyond lumpy aliens, mad scientists and laser guns. **Brainstorm** offers us images of Heaven, government corruption and a love story and in doing so offers us almost too much, leading to a confusion of agenda, but still remains a limited success. **Brainstorm** is rarely screened now, a nearly lost oddity of science fiction cinema, but its influence remains, from the comic book hi-tech of **The Matrix** to the virtual reality rollercoaster theme park rides of Trumbull's own design.

'THE DEAD ZONE'

David Cronenberg's **The Dead Zone** (1983) opens quietly. After teaching his English classes for the day, John Smith takes his girlfriend Sarah, also a teacher, to the Castle Rock fair[1]. While on the rollercoaster, he experiences strange head pains. He takes Sarah back to her house but twice turns down her offer for him to spend the night – "Better not" – although he does promise to marry her.

It's a rainy night, and we see a tired lorry driver take a corner badly and lose control of the vehicle. The container is now blocking the road, and Smith sees it only too late, ploughing his car into its side.

Smith is admitted to, and wakes up in, the Weizak Institute. It is a bleak winter – as it is in all subsequent scenes. Sam Weizak, his doctor, allows Smith's parents to visit him, and he learns that he has been in a coma for five years. In this time his mother has become a religious fanatic, convinced that her son's recovery is a literal miracle, and his girlfriend has married another man and had a child, Denny.

Smith grabs the arm of a nurse attending him and has the first of his visions – he sees that her house is burning and that her daughter is in danger. He tells her that it is not too late to save her, and the child is duly saved – his prediction was correct. When his ex-girlfriend comes to see him, she asks him about his precognitive abilities, which are now the talk of Castle Rock. He decides to hold a news conference, in which one TV reporter challenges him to prove his skills by demonstration. Smith explains that he has to touch his subject for any result, and the reporter duly offers his arm. The resulting scene so alarms the reporter that he struggles to leave, uttering the immortal line, "Get away from me, you fucking freak!" His mother watches the altercation on TV and suffers a heart attack. She dies soon after.

Smith moves out of the Weizak Institute to stay with his father. He receives a visit from the local sheriff, Bannerman, who asks him to help solve a series of murders. He refuses. Later, after being visited by his ex-girlfriend, he sees Bannerman asking for help on television in the wake of yet another murder. He decides to try, but initial efforts prove fruitless. While he's with the sheriff, another murder is reported. They go to the scene of the crime, where Smith touches the body. He now "sees" the events leading up to the murder and the face of the killer – it is the sheriff's deputy, Dodd. Smith and Bannerman go to Dodd's house, where they find that he has killed himself[2]. Dodd's mother shoots Smith in the arm before being shot herself by Bannerman.

Weizak visits Smith at home, and asks him to return to the Institute. Despite the fact that his health is deteriorating, he refuses. He accepts the job of tutoring Chris, the son of Roger Stuart, a very successful local

businessman. Upon arriving at Stuart's home he meets Greg Stillson, a politician on a fundraising trip. Stuart astutely warns Smith of Stillson's more reprehensible qualities, and we then see Stillson blackmailing a newspaper editor critical of his campaign[3].

Smith's tutoring of Chris goes well, although he is visited while teaching at home by a Stillson campaigner, who turns out to be his ex-girlfriend's husband. Smith later has a vision of Chris and other boys drowning, although he has a sense that it's not too late to prevent. He sees that Stuart plans an ice-hockey game for his son's friends, and begs him to call it off. Stuart initially refuses and only capitulates as a ruse to get Smith out of the house, his position as Chris's tutor terminated. Stuart asks Chris to join the other boys, but he is scared and refuses. Needless to say, Smith is vindicated – the ice breaks and a number of boys drown.

When a Stillson parade takes place outside his house, Smith goes out looking for his ex-girlfriend, knowing that she is involved in the campaign. As he searches for her, Stillson passes, shaking hands. Smith takes Stillson's hand and has a vision of Stillson as President initiating a nuclear strike on Russia.

Weizak visits Smith again. Smith explains that some visions are incomplete, and that there is a grey area, a "dead zone" when the outcome can be changed. He asks Weizak if he would kill Hitler, if he could go back in time and meet him as a young man, prior to the birth of the Nazi party. Weizak states that he would. Smith therefore decides to kill Stillson, and narration is provided during the following scenes of a letter he has left for Sarah explaining his actions.

He hides overnight with a rifle in the balcony of a hall in which Stillson is to speak. When Stillson takes the stand Smith stands up but is distracted by Sarah's shouting "Johnny!" He misses Stillson and is shot himself by Stillson's bodyguard. He raises the gun again but Stillson has taken Denny and holds the baby in front of him for protection. Smith hesitates and is shot again by the bodyguard – he falls from the balcony. Stillson approaches, asking who sent him, and Smith grabs his arm; he "sees" a copy of *Time*, the image of Stillson holding Denny on its cover, and a weary Stillson committing suicide. Smith is happy, his destiny fulfilled, and holds Sarah in his arms as he dies.

1.

The loneliness and the melancholy and the impossibility of dealing with things. And yet the necessity to do it. That's what it was. It's Chris Walken's face. That's the subject of the movie; that's what the movie was about. All the things that are in his face. That's difficult to write about.[4]

Cronenberg's unremittingly bleak adaptation of Stephen King's *The Dead Zone*, whose grimness should be clear from the above synopsis, was instrumental in the subsequent success of Christopher Walken's career, providing one of his first starring roles and setting the template for many of his performances for years to come. He is John Smith, a regular guy, an endearingly vague English teacher with his hair combed down and his duffel-coat buttoned tight; he is John Smith, ashen-faced freak, neurasthenic cheekbones framed by spiky hair, barely seen after the accident without his trademark long, batwing black coat. It's virtually the defining change in Walken's career, this transition from normal to different, from insider to outsider, and his low-key mastery of the change is central to the film's success. The film also laid the groundwork for the iconic use of Walken's face in subsequent films: as a shortcut to ideas of strangeness and supranormality, involving an almost pornographic lingering on his features.

There is an undefinable and irreducible quality to Walken's face, expressive not only of strangeness but of a sophistication beyond the reach of ordinary mortals. In this way he's become something of a Hollywood-friendly Klaus Kinski, and has run the risk of being typecast in "weird" roles in which his only brief would be "do Chris Walken". Fortunately he hasn't yet

taken this easy route, unlike such self-parodic actors as Robert de Niro and Dennis Hopper – in fact he insists he's always wanted to play comedy roles. To my mind he's missed his ideal calling, though; imagine Walken playing opposite Eastwood and Kinski in a Sergio Leone western[5].

The other films in Walken's canon closest to **The Dead Zone** are **Communion** (1989) and **Brainstorm** (1983), as both involve Walken as a sympathetic character undergoing paranormal or transpersonal experiences. In **Communion** he plays Whitley Strieber, a SF/horror author who is abducted by aliens. Strieber is a real writer (the 1981 film **Wolfen** is based on one of his books) and the book *Communion* was enormously popular on publication[6]. The film didn't do particularly well, despite being released at one of UFO-mania's many peaks – perhaps images of Walken salsa-dancing with greys were just too bizarre for the average viewer. **Brainstorm** fared a little better. Directed by SFX expert Douglas Trumbull, it's an early VR film along the lines of Kathryn Bigelow's **Strange Days** (1995). Walken plays an eccentric but likeable scientist involved in the development of a technology enabling one person's experiences to be recorded for playback by another. As ever, the scientist takes it too far, recording death experiences in an attempt to discover what lies beyond mortality.

2.

Critics have often complained of poorly cast male leads in Cronenberg films, and the entirely forgettable protagonists of such early efforts as **Shivers**, **The Brood** and **Scanners** would seem to support this. But take James Woods in **Videodrome**, Jeremy Irons in **Dead Ringers**, Jeff Goldblum in **The Fly** and here Christopher Walken in **The Dead Zone**: each of these performances are arguably the best in the respective actors' careers, and it's worth noting that some have marked the actors' transitions to A-list stars. Jeremy Irons, receiving an Oscar for **Reversal Of Fortune**, even thanked David Cronenberg rather than the director of **Reversal...**

It's worth noting that the protagonists of the earlier films represent agents of order, powerless in the face of biological revolt; their very blandness is a function of their character, and the viewer is not really encouraged to sympathise with them. The leads in the latter films have by contrast integrated the classic horror genre theme of conflict between established order and the repressed/the Other – here the protagonists are themselves the monsters.

This oversimplifies the situation in **The Dead Zone** a little, however. While Smith is certainly "Other", the Martin Sheen character Greg Stillson is the true monster of the film. Smith and Stillson are portrayed as being two sides of the same coin. While Smith is tall, blond and introverted, Stillson is short and stocky, dark and gregarious. Even their acting styles seem diametrically opposed – Walken subtly plays a man for whom emotional coldness is the only way to deal with life, while Sheen looks like he's just stepped off the **Dr Strangelove** set. Stillson however has visions, just like Smith. His serve no philanthropic function, though, existing purely to feed his ambition: "I have had a vision that I am going to be President of the United States someday, and I have accepted that responsibility..."

Stillson later recounts the reasons why he is about to launch a nuclear attack on Russia: "In the middle of the night it came to me. I must get up now – right now – and fulfil my destiny."

Conversely, Smith's visions help people, by and large. He saves the lives of the nurse's son and Chris Stuart, discovers the identity of the Castle Rock killer and averts a nuclear catastrophe. His one "selfish" use of the power, during the news conference, results in his mother's heart attack. It's important that there's no self-aggrandising motive behind his actions, unlike those of Stillson. But his initial visions mark him as a social pariah, for all their life-saving qualities, and subsequent ones force him out of a job (Chris Stuart) and ultimately to his death (Greg Stillson). Pleasure is denied Smith from the moment he falls into his coma, and there's a sense in which the repression he undergoes – the denial of his need to love and be loved, to experience sexual contact, to be accepted – somehow strengthens his powers.

3.

The signal induces a brain tumour in the viewer. It's the tumour that creates the hallucinations.
—Videodrome

The Dead Zone, while key in accounts of Walken's acting career, is usually glossed over in critiques of Cronenberg's films in favour of the films more clearly fitting his "body horror" schematic, especially considering that its release closely followed that of **Videodrome** (1983), probably his most accomplished and complex work. In some ways it is itself a precognitive effort, foreshadowing Cronenberg's concentration since the late '80s on literary adaptations[7] – with the exception of the obscure **Fast Company**, prior to working on **The Dead Zone** Cronenberg had written the original screenplays or at least generated the original ideas for all of his films. It's true that Cronenberg wanted to work on a less personal project following the intensity of **Videodrome**, but also that he wanted to defy expectation, especially in the wake of so many poor King adaptations: "I was confident that I could find a version of *The Dead Zone* that would completely satisfy me, challenge me, and that would *be* me."[8]

In fact the film is in many ways classic Cronenberg, and the differences between this and his other films of the period are also instructive.

It's undeniably far less visceral than his other films. In the Stephen

King novel John Smith has a brain tumour. It's not clear whether, as above, the tumour causes the visions or the other way around, but no mention of a tumour is made in the film, despite the fact that ideas of "the new flesh" are a key Cronenberg concern. Most of his films prior to **The Dead Zone** had dealt with the idea of mutation – of people often trying to find positive effects for their biological revolt. John Smith's shift in reaction to his precognitive ability – from seeing it as a "curse" to seeing it as a "gift" – fits this theme perfectly. The theme of disease is present in the film – each of Smith's visions ages him and brings him closer to death – but the use of an actual mutation would seem to be more in line with Cronenberg's other work.

It's possible though that it was felt that, as well as being too close to **Videodrome**, the tumour might work against the thematic consistency of this particular film. While most Cronenberg films operate in a secular universe in which science has replaced a Christian God, **The Dead Zone** appears in many ways to be a religious film, or at least one principally concerned with ideas of fate and destiny:

*The folks in **The Dead Zone** tend to be God-fearing characters, whereas in my other films they are not. Because many of the scientists in my early films are absent from the films themselves, although their influence remains, I think you could make a good case for saying that in **The Dead Zone**, God is the scientist whose experiments are not always working out and that the Johnny Smith character is one of his failed experiments.[9]*

While Smith is in a coma his mother becomes deeply religious. She claims that his eventual recovery is a literal miracle. Others then see his powers in these terms, despite the fact that such abilities do not easily sit with Christian ideology. Sherriff Bannerman tells Smith, while attempting to persuade him to help solve the Castle Rock killings, that: "If God has seen fit to bless you with this gift, you should use it."

While Smith could use his power for personal gain – the mountain of mail he amasses demonstrates that his powers are very much in demand – he doesn't. He lives in straitened circumstances and is near-celibate: during the last of his ex-girlfriend's visits they have sex, but the finality of the event only serves to reinforce his emotional isolation. He is, as we have already seen, self-sacrificing throughout, and becomes convinced that it is his destiny to stop Stillson from becoming President, even if he loses his own life in the process. All of this, along with the simple fact of the visions themselves, gives Smith a messianic quality – he is a prophet, and can easily be seen, within the framework of the film, as a Christ figure.

The near-celibacy is important also in placing **The Dead Zone** alongside Cronenberg's other films. Critics and fans have seen the apparent lack of sexual disgust – again a key Cronenberg theme – in the film as marking it as inauthentic. A sexual theme is in the film, though, albeit one marked by the conspicuous absence of sexuality throughout. The one sex scene paradoxically reinforces this idea – it's a taste of what Smith has missed out on, and what he can never have, and as such seems immeasurably cruel. The film is characterised by slow, lingering and passionless shots, cold landscapes populated by heavily clothed people. Most of the speed and action we see occurs during Smith's visions – with one notable exception. The scene of Dodd's suicide is graphic and disturbing, as he forces his head down on to a pair of scissors fixed to a bathroom sink. These same scissors have been used in the Castle Rock killings, which have a sexual element – in both instances penetration is brutal, bloody and ends in death. This is however virtually the only kind of sexuality with which Smith will be even tangentially involved – dysfunctional, cold and psychotic.

The winter settings throughout the film serve minimal plot function – the ice-hockey accident is their only purpose in purely narrative terms – but in terms of atmosphere they are crucial, acting as an indicator of Smith's emotional and sexual condition:

*Sexuality doesn't surface in **The Dead Zone** in the same way it does in my other films, but it's certainly there. It's a very repressed, restrained and frustrated thing.*[10]

But as before, there is a sense in which the denial of Smith's pleasure, his circumstantial asceticism, focuses his energies – in order to help other people he must reject worldly pleasures himself.

4.

It was pleasing that a lot of critics said it was the first Stephen King movie that faithfully translated the novel. Amusing, because we threw a lot out. There was no attempt to slavishly reproduce it. But somehow the tone... There was a tone to the book that did strike me and I distilled it out.[11]

The Dead Zone is probably still the most critically acclaimed adaptation of a Stephen King novel. The competition, while not thin on the ground, has been dire, with only **Carrie** (1976), **Misery** (1990), **The Shining** (1980) and **The Shawshank Redemption** (1994) being anything more than entry-level efforts. The film wasn't particularly successful commercially, and it's possible that its lacklustre performance was due to its bleakness and intensely downbeat tone – too depressing to be a date movie and not gory enough to satisfy most horror fans, especially at a time of increasing reliance on grisly effects work. But it did provide both Cronenberg – hitherto reviled by most serious critics – and Walken with critical acceptability and a platform from which to go on to more successful work.

The film also deserves closer attention than it has received from critics writing about Cronenberg. Most critics tend to have an exclusive focus on films fitting relatively narrow, auteurist views of the director, rather than an inclusive focus dealing with all of his work. While **Fast Company** and his TV work are by all accounts unremarkable, **The Dead Zone** is not, and Cronenberg's own thoughts about the film are far from dismissive – a critical re-evaluation is long overdue.

NOTES

1. Castle Rock is the setting of most of Stephen King's fiction, and John Smith's home town.

2. The admittedly grisly suicide scene has been snipped from most UK video prints of the film. **The Dead Zone** received an 18 certificate, despite the fact that this missing scene is the only violent incident in the narrative. James Ferman once boasted of never wanting to cut a Cronenberg film, and it's possible that the scene has been restored in a video re-release.

3. This is one of the only scenes in the film not presented from John Smith's viewpoint, giving it a disorienting quality.

4. *Cronenberg On Cronenberg*, ed. Chris Rodley, Faber & Faber 1992, p.111.

5. He actually came closest when appearing in **Last Man Standing**, the remake of Leone's **A Fistful Of Dollars**.

6. A background in SF and fantasy fiction seems almost a prerequisite for setting up non-standard belief systems these days. L. Ron Hubbard, the founder of the massively popular Church of Scientology, which also involves belief in the malign influence of alien lifeforms, enjoyed a mediocre career as a writer of SF before hitting on his true calling. Strieber has written a sequel to *Communion* which apparently makes the first book look staid by comparison, and is a respected figure on the UFO lecture circuit.

7. Aside from this being an adaptation of a Stephen King novel, there are other important literary references within the film. Washington Irving's story *The Legend Of Sleepy Hollow* is referred to a number of times, and Walken in fact resembles Ichabod Crane, protagonist of the story, with his loping gait and grim demeanour. But **The Dead Zone** actually bears more resemblance to another Irving story, *Rip Van Winkle*, adapted from a German folk tale – here the protagonist goes to sleep for twenty years and awakens to discover a world which he no longer recognises. References to Poe's poetry also feature in the film, and while this is in keeping with Smith's character – he is an English teacher, and Poe is a key writer in the American literary canon – Poe's obsession with resurrection and the paranormal make this unlikely to have been an arbitrary choice. Incidentally, Walken has since played the headless horseman in Tim Burton's film of **The Legend Of Sleepy Hollow** (1999).

8. *Cronenberg On Cronenberg* p.110.

9. ibid p.111.

10. ibid p.111.

11. ibid p.116.

LOVING THE ALIEN:
'THE COMFORT OF STRANGERS'

My father was a very big man. All his life he wore a black moustache. When it turned grey he used a little brush to keep it black, such as ladies use for their eyes. "Mascara". Everyone was afraid of him – my mother, my four sisters. At the dining table, you could not speak until spoken to first by my father. But he loved me. I was his favourite.

(Robert, **The Comfort Of Strangers**)

Compared to, say, Robert De Niro or Harvey Keitel, Christopher Walken has enjoyed only a small window of opportunity as a film star. Granted, in his thirties, the wall eyes, parchment skin and impossibly sculpted hair suggested a youthful delicacy, a haunted vulnerability that made him – momentarily – a marketably tragic figure. But come the 1980s and his passage into middle age, and Walken's looks began to harden. The actor became more and more the alien creature, his increasingly intractable strangeness channelled by the decade following into a series of monologue-ing cameos interrupted only by the occasional eccentric *tour de force* – of which Donald Cammell's **Wild Side** (1995) is perhaps the most notable example.

The Comfort Of Strangers (1990) is a film that sits Janus-faced in Walken's career. Directed by Paul Schrader from Harold Pinter's adaptation of Ian McEwan's novel, it embraces the two images of Walken, flirting with the human depths plumbed in **The Deer Hunter** (1979) and **The Dead Zone** (1983) while exploiting the essential alienness, the unknowability, of later roles. Unknowability is, in fact, the very subject of the picture. The story of troubled English lovers who, while holidaying in Venice, are befriended then destroyed by a suave local couple, **The Comfort Of Strangers** constructs a chill parallel between tourism and romance, the message of which is that each of us, in the final analysis, is agonisingly alone. To quote Cesare Pavese (as does McEwan in the opening to the book), "Travelling is a brutality. It forces you to trust strangers and to lose sight of all that familiar comfort of home and friends", and the suspicion throughout the movie is that the feigned intimacies inevitable when we venture abroad are comparable to the pretence of closeness that exists between too many couples, likewise once strangers to each other.

As the force who rends the English pair in two, Walken could not be better cast. A strangely ageless, sexless devil with motives that seem permanently obscure, the actor here appears mystery incarnate, "as creepy" (as David Thomson puts it) "as fog"[1]. At the same time, however, the film mischievously toys with the notion that Walken's is the character with whom

we should most identify, carefully deploying the human shading of which he is capable. The end result is all the more painfully insightful in consequence, tantalising us with the promise of an understanding, of a psychological intimacy, that remains forever just beyond our reach.

Venice. English tourists Colin Mayhew (Rupert Everett) and Mary Kenway (Natasha Richardson) are revisiting the city in an attempt to rekindle their relationship. Both seem bored; Mary has two children by a former partner, and Colin seems unwilling to commit.

On a visit to a glassworks in Morano, Colin spies the Armani-suited Robert (Christopher Walken). Later that night, lost in Venice and looking for somewhere to eat, Colin and Mary chance upon Robert again. He takes them to a bar where he treats them to wine, breadsticks and faintly perverse stories of his diplomat father, mother, sisters and Canadian wife. On leaving, Mary is unwell, and the couple end up sleeping in the street.

The next day, still not having returned to their hotel, Colin and Mary are intercepted by Robert at a café. Despite initial doubts, they accept an invitation to his sumptuous apartment. They spend the day sleeping, and awake to find their clothes have disappeared. Mary goes in search of them and meets Robert's wife Caroline (Helen Mirren), who explains that they are being laundered. She confesses that she watched the pair as they slept, and reveals that the bar to which Robert took them is actually owned by her husband.

Returning from business, Robert opens a bottle of champagne and shows Colin the books and objects favoured by his father and grandfather. When Colin suggests the palazzo is a museum to their memory, Robert assaults him. At dinner, Colin objects to Robert's support of Britain's right wing government. The couple leave – but not before Caroline begs them to return, whispering that she is a prisoner.

Back at the hotel, Colin and Mary discover a new passion for each other, and make love repeatedly. On a restaurant terrace, all eyes are on the couple as they eat. Later, they exchange Sadean sexual fantasies. When Mary wakes from a nightmare, she reveals that, while at Robert's flat, she glimpsed a surreptitiously taken photograph of Colin.

The next day, on the beach, Colin tells Mary about Robert punching him. When Mary returns from a swim, he suggests that, back in England, they move in together, but this time it's she who is hesitant. The couple take a cruiser back to their hotel, but decide at the last moment to leave the boat for a shortcut by foot. They alight close to Robert's apartment and, hailed by Caroline from a window, decide to pay Robert and Caroline a final visit.

Robert informs the couple that he and Caroline are moving to Canada, and that he left a message at the hotel asking them to call by before their departure. While Caroline makes Mary some tea, the men walk to the bar, which Robert is in the process of selling. Along the way, he greets several locals in Italian. Later, he explains he was telling them that Colin was his lover, and that Caroline was jealous because she is attracted to Colin too. When Colin asks about the photograph, Robert simply points out the barber shop used by his father, grandfather and him, and the cemetery which now houses his forebears.

At the apartment, Caroline tells the drugged Mary how her back was injured in a sadistic sexual game played with Robert. She leads Mary into the bedroom – its walls lined with pictures of Colin. She remembers how excited Robert was by his first glimpse of the Englishman, and the way in which Colin became a shared obsession that brought them closer together.

Robert and Colin return. As Mary looks on, incapable of intervention, Robert cuts Colin's throat with a straight razor after Caroline kisses the tourist's mouth, which she has smeared with her own blood.

At the police station, Mary is at a loss to explain the nature of her relationship with Robert and Caroline. She tells the officers that she and Colin were to be married. Bemused by the trail of incriminating evidence he appears not to have been bothered to hide, the police also quiz Robert. But in answer to their questions, Robert replies with a memory of his father – of how, when his moustache turned grey, he used to colour it with mascara...

An Italian-British co-production also known as **Cortesie Per Gli Ospiti, The Comfort Of Strangers** was made under the aegis of London's Sovereign Pictures – a company specialising in unlikely international confections. With a Cannes première in mind (the film did indeed close the 1990 festival), former Fellini producer Angelo Rizzoli first approached Pinter to adapt McEwan's 1981 third novel, then took the project to Schrader, intending – in the words of the director – "to protect [himself] from an overly polite adaptation. They wanted an American who could mix it up a little bit with Harold"[2]. Though Schrader's directorial career was founded on his scriptwriting, Pinter's vision was scrupulously adhered to, read-throughs with the actors resulting in the modification of only "four or five lines"[3]. McEwan also seemed happy to defer to Pinter's authority. On a visit to Rome's Pathé studios (formerly Dino De Laurentiis' Cinecittà rival Dinocittà) to view the shooting of interiors, he commented: "I've done enough film work to know you'll be disappointed if you look for a version of your novel. It's just a catalyst... The story tries to align intellectual notions of freedom and sexual desire. There's a dissonance between the head and the heart that's part of the novel – but not part of the film."[4]

On first viewing, **The Comfort Of Strangers** exhibits a desultoriness partly the result of its several hands: while the sexual antagonism is McEwan's, the issues of language, power and (political) extremism are very much Pinter's and the theme of isolation Schrader's. Or, as Schrader himself put it: "One of the things I'm most proud of about the film is that it does not obscure the signature of either Ian McEwan or Harold Pinter. You can see Ian's sensibility, and Harold's sensibility and my sensibility, and therefore it has that richness."[5] The disconnected quality of the movie is, of course, also relevant to its overriding interest in the disconnectedness of people, and to this end the uncharacteristic roles adopted by its creators are provocative, with Schrader the screenwriter giving way to a playwright adapting another's novel.

The taking on of unfamiliar guises extends to the look of the picture too, with Schrader pushing Michael Mann's regular photographer Dante Spinotti to depart from "a postcard view of Venice which you see when you close your eyes"[6]. The upshot – sun-drenched squares alternating with a cosmetic nocturnal warren that houses both Robert's neon-lit bar and one spectacularly odd aqua-blue shop window described by Colin as "look[ing] like a space shuttle" – seems more akin to the alien exotica of a Tangier, Cairo or Istanbul. The effect is reinforced by Angelo Badalamenti's swooning score, a blend of the operatic with the north African, and makes perfect sense of Schrader's decision not to use Venice for the interiors or night-time scenes. A suspicion of artificiality dogs both the tourists' evening odysseys and Robert's plush palazzo (featuring as it does a balcony that's surely inside rather than out and sunset views that are too perfect to be real), turning Venice into a set of claustrophobic mental cages rather a major First World city. Lost in the maze one night, Colin is taken aback by a glazier trundling through the Venetian alleyways, but in this place of imprisoning invisible walls maybe the encounter should have come as no surprise. As Mary says the following morning, "It's like a prison here", a far more accurate observation than her tourist guff on first entering Robert's bar: "It's the real Venice".

Most importantly perhaps, this sense of slippage – of people and places not quite as they should be – carries over into the very casting of the film. Significantly, the only member of the troupe not at odds with herself is Natasha Richardson – member of the famous English acting clan who, having previously starred in another Schrader for-hire job, **Patty Hearst** (1988), here *plays* an English actress even glimpsed in one scene reading Kenneth Branagh's autobiography. For the rest, Rupert Everett – homosexual in real life – plays a straight man hounded by Italians who repeatedly impugn his sexuality; Helen Mirren (the Essex-born granddaughter of a White Russian nobleman) essays a Canadian exile; and native New Yorker Walken is tasked with the job of a Venetian who speaks English as if it were some unusual, expensive wine to be rolled over the palate before being lip-smackingly expelled.

Walken's character is the chief means by which Schrader and Pinter wrest the movie from its literary source. In the novel, Robert is archetypal Mediterranean macho, short and squat with a cheap shirt open to the waist to expose chest hair and a gold chain. In the film, by contrast, he's an elegant aristo whose exquisite apartment – a triumph of Gianni Quaranta's production design – screams of the burden of family privilege; it is perhaps only the way Walken wears his double-breasted Armani (hands thrust deep into jacket pockets, crumpling it around his waist) that connects this tasteful creature with the tacky Latin lover of the book. The decision to transform Robert so seems to have been taken in part to ally **The Comfort Of Strangers** with those other movies that draw upon Venice's morbid atmosphere of liquefaction – notably Nicolas Roeg's **Don't Look Now** (1973), with its cultivated art restorer protagonists, and Luchino Visconti's **Death In Venice** (1971), in which a white-suited Dirk Bogarde finds salvation in gay voyeurism. (Though Venice pervades McEwan's text, it's never mentioned by name.) Equally important, however, is the way this reinvention allows Robert

to bear the weight of the past by placing upon him the pressures of an ancient family. His recollections of childhood and, specifically, of his formidable diplomat father are entirely Pinter's, and make Robert the film's enigmatic key rather than the cipher of destruction he is for McEwan.

Thus it is that while Everett and Richardson *appear* to take centre stage, the movie constantly distracts itself with thoughts of Walken; as an audience, we constantly find ourselves drawn to him just as Everett and Richardson themselves are drawn for the strangely fatalistic finale. The first words we hear in the film, as the camera glides caressingly through Robert's apartment, is a voice-over from Walken relating the anecdote of the mascara brush. Though we never actually see who speaks, he is held up – however fleetingly – as the narrator, our way into what follows. And even after Robert has been established as a figure of shadowy malevolence, the film maintains an addiction for him – most peculiarly in the scene where Everett and Richardson leave after the strained dinner party which follows Robert's unexpected assault upon the Englishman. By this point Walken and Mirren's motives have become diabolically obscure, and one would expect Schrader's camera to leave with the bewildered couple. But instead it lingers for a few perturbing beats on Walken's side of the door, just as, later, it will return as Walken packs away the family heirlooms, prefiguring the last visit of the tourists themselves.

On first being assigned **The Comfort Of Strangers**, it was suggested that Schrader consider Klaus Maria Brandauer and Charlotte Rampling for the parts of Robert and Caroline. His reply? "Yeah, well, they walk on screen and everyone shouts 'It's the Addams Family', and where do you go from there? It is all over. The trick for Christopher Walken is to be charming, not evil. The evil of Robert will come through."[7] Sure enough, it's Walken's ability as a charmer that lends the movie its mysterious dynamism. We hang on his every, exquisitely formed word – caring little about Mary's simpering after her absent children or Colin's vain preenings in front of the bathroom mirror – when, still existing only in voice-over, he begins a tale of vengeance enacted on him by his sisters for confessing a game of dress-up with their mother's clothes. And, just like Colin and Mary adrift in the city, we are eager to follow this urbane Samaritan when he finally does appear in the flesh, and are even prepared to ignore the dubious male clientele of the bar (not to mention the fact that, contrary to expectations, there is no food), so seductive a character is he. Agreed, when Robert has finished his story of being fed laxative and puking and shitting in his father's study, we may briefly concur with the tourists that this is "a truly terrible man". But the couple's reaction stems mostly from English reserve in the face of someone (as Robert himself says) "of passionate curiosity", and they like we will once more be compelled to follow come the next meeting.

Robert's allure derives partly from his social standing, mainly from Walken's immense skill at flattering us with glimpses of an inner life; take, for example, the wonderful laugh of remembrance and regret he gives on recalling his father's question when the soiled young boy is discovered ("Robert, have you been eating chocolate?"). Even the wink he proffers Colin after punching him violently in the stomach feels like the sharing of some subtle confidence, and once within his orbit Colin and Mary's lives seem vibrantly renewed, as if their self-belief has been boosted by association with such a fascinating individual; the pair suddenly and passionately share the same bed again, and the book Colin has been asked to edit by his publisher – and which at the beginning of the movie he finds "unreadable" – is returned to with fresh vigour. Invitations to read Robert prove similarly irresistible as the movie proceeds. Little wonder that the police marvel at the amount of incriminating evidence he leaves, for throughout the film he teases us with lavish clues to his personality, going so far as to explain that, in order to explain how he met his wife he must first talk about his father, and to lay out ancestral objects on a table in the palazzo. The central exhibit is, however, the tale of the mascara, expertly repeated by Walken thrice over.

With each repetition of the mascara story, increased scrutiny is brought to bear upon its speaker. In the first instance, he is merely a voice. The second time, yes, we see him in person, but the camera pans away first to dally with the bar's male patrons, and then – lest we've jumped to any conclusions – to spend just enough time with the female customers to undermine our suspicions of what kind of establishment this is. Only on the third occasion do we stay with Walken. In the wake of the murder, our clear understanding of the bar's gay users and Robert's apparent proclamation that Colin is his lover, the camera inches slowly in. Our attention ratcheted up to an intolerable pitch, with the last word, "mascara!", the movie ends.

The assumption inevitably is that Robert is a tortured homosexual, but it's Walken's talent to leave question marks hanging. Certainly, the mascara detail feminises an image of uncomplicated maleness ("My father and his father understood themselves clearly. They were men, and they were proud of their sex") and seems bound up with the character's ostentatious hatred of freedoms which would allow for the activities of "communist poofs". But what "the brush... such as ladies use" really represents is the fallibility of the old order, a single imperfection which throws Robert's cool, serried world off its axis into a torment of self-doubt, dysfunction and nihilistic isolation. In this maelstrom, love is nothing to do with respect and connection, but is rather a passive, masochistic state in which the participants can only come together by finding a common object of abuse. The fact that Walken has the discipline to show us so much and no more is what makes his performance in **The Comfort Of Strangers** among his most painfully human to date.

NOTES

1. *A Biographical Dictionary Of Film*, Andre Deutsch, rev. ed. 1994, p.786.

2. "Following The Tour Guide" by Jonathan Romney, *Monthly Film Bulletin*, vol.58 no.684, January 1991, p.6.

3. Harold Pinter in "From The Terrace" by Deborah Auld, *Village Voice*, 12 December 1989.

4. ibid.

5. "Following The Tour Guide" by Jonathan Romney, *Monthly Film Bulletin*, vol.58 no.684, January 1991, p.6.

6. "Sadistic Games Of Death And Venice" by Chris Peachment, *The Times*, 1990.

7. ibid.

'COMMUNION': ALIEN TERRITORY

There are an awful lot of things to dislike about **Communion** (1989), the allegedly true account of author Whitley Strieber's abduction by alien life forms. For one thing, the movie was made by Philippe Mora, who you might remember as the director of such films as **The Return Of Captain Invincible** and **Pterodactyl Woman From Beverly Hills**. For another, it was produced and adapted for the screen by Strieber, a writer whose sole claim to fame before he began bleating on about UFOs was that he wrote **The Hunger**, a decidedly average novel that was turned into a decidedly average movie by Tony Scott. And then there's the appalling sub-**Close Encounters** electronic score, the interminable fantasy sequences, the very average special fx and an Eric Clapton theme that's so soporific one assumes Slowhand was either using way too much heroin or nowhere near enough. And yet, for its many, many flaws, there is one thing that makes **Communion** an essential video purchase. And his name is Christopher Walken.

Rather appropriately, **Communion** finds Walken in alien territory. But it isn't the sci-fi subject matter that's atypical; by 1989, Walken was already the veteran of fantasy pictures like **Brainstorm** and **The Dead Zone**. What makes **Communion** so special is that it features Christopher Walken playing a part that many people assumed to be beyond him; that of a regular guy.

Throughout his typecast career, Christopher Walken has always suggested that he might possess something actually approaching range. Besides his all-singing, all-dancing turn in **Pennies From Heaven**, he was superbly tongue-in-cheek in **Pulp Fiction**, **Mousehunt** and **Wayne's World II**, and he once came within a whisker of landing the Ryan O'Neal roll in **Love Story** (You can you just see him delivering the eulogy at Ali MacGraw's funeral: "She... LOVED Mozart, the Beatles... AND *me!*"). Then, of course, there are his string of appearances on *Saturday Night Live* during which he has done everything from sending up his own movies like **The Dead Zone** (he played a man who could predict trivial future events like paper cuts) to, on one particularly outstanding Christmas special, performing a five-minute festive medley of "Frosty The Snowman" and "Walken In A Winter Wonderland".

And then there's *Saturday Zoo*. If you had a social life in the early '90s, you probably never saw Jonathan Ross's short-lived variety series. If, like me, you didn't, then you might have been lucky enough to catch Walken's appearance live. Picture the scene: the lights come up to reveal Christopher Walken sat in a wicker chair, wearing a *loud* jumper and clutching a book of fairy stories. "Hello, children," he smiles, before embarking on a Mafiaapproved retelling of the story of the three little pigs. "In the village there was a wolf. A big wolf. Bad wolf. Big bad wolf. Get the picture." The tale then heats up; "Exit pig one. Pig two, same story. 'I'll huff I'll puff and I'll blow your house down.' *Arriverderci, porco numero due. Buon giorno, salami.*" It was an inspired bit of television and one that proved that, as well as effortless intensity and a reptilian stare, Christopher Walken had a sense of humour – and, as such, was as well qualified to play normal as the next guy (providing the next guy wasn't Ted Bundy).

Not that Whitley Strieber, in Walken's hands at any rate, is your everyday Hollywood dad. What with his penchant for writing in his fedora, cowboy boots and underpants and his habit of video taping everything from his son's Halloween party to himself at his word processor, Strieber would be considered a grade-A fruitcake by most people's standards. Compared to some of the freak-shows Walken has been called upon to play, the writer is but mildly eccentric. And even with all his foibles, Strieber gives Walken the chance to do things you never thought you'd see him perform on film. Indeed, for anyone raised on the familiar image of Walken brandishing a handgun and a sneer, there is something quite shocking about the sight of him reading a child a bedtime story.

Communion was the last in a series of "family entertainments" Christopher Walken made during the late 1980s. Other films in this cycle included the inoffensive Robert Redford-directed **The Milagro Beanfield War** and the Matthew Broderick vehicle **Biloxi Blues**. Seeing that it contains the most anal probing you'll find this side of the *South Park* pilot episode, you might be forgiven for thinking that the only family **Communion** would be suitable for was Charles Manson's. For all its guff about God and alien visitation, **Communion** is at its most successful as a study of a family trying to hold itself together. And it's as a father trying to prevent his "unique" experience from ruining his happy home life that Walken's performance succeeds every bit as well as his spine-chilling turns in **King Of New York**, **The Comfort Of Strangers** and **True Romance**.

From the moment Whitley Strieber burns a family meal, you know **Communion** isn't going to be your average Christopher Walken movie. In truth, it takes quite a long time to adjust to the sight of Walken as a loving husband and father. The memories of Vincenzo Coccetti and Frank White are so powerful that you can't help but read something sinister into acts as innocent as Strieber wishing his boy "good night" or demanding a kiss from the kid on his return from school (the fact that the latter request is followed with "Is there something wrong with you?" doesn't add to the tenderness of the moment). The criminal credentials that make it hard to see Walken as anything other than a hood are but part of the baggage this extraordinary actor brings to every movie he makes. The same goes for his unique speech patterns (always effective but never affected) and unusual gait (always deliberate but never exaggerated). Walken's idiosyncrasies insist that Whitley Strieber be the superficial spit of his other screen personas. It's only once you scratch beneath the surface that the character's unique qualities can be appreciated. And it's only once you've finished digging, that you can appreciate Strieber as amongst Christopher Walken's most fully realised screen creations.

Communion opens on a night-time view of the South Manhattan skyline. It's an interesting shot, particularly since we're not used to seeing New York from this perspective. It also represents the summit of director Philippe Mora's achievement and innovation. As you might expect from the man who made **Howling II ... Your Sister Is A Werewolf**, Mora is a real bread-and-butter, point-and-shoot merchant. His talent is so limited that even when he does try something different (the first scene in the psychiatrist's office is partially shot from the ceiling) the effect draws attention to itself rather than adds anything to the film. None of this should bother us, however, since **Communion** isn't Mora's movie, it's Christopher Walken's.

Walken plays Whitley Strieber, a man who exists, more or less, in the real world. He has a fairly regular job, he likes to spend time with his wife (Lindsay Crouse) and child (Joel Carlson) and he enjoys weekend trips to his country retreat. It's during one such excursion that the event that will turn Strieber's life upside down takes place. With the family's holiday cottage immersed in the sort of god-light Spielberg overdosed on in **Close Encounters**, something enters Strieber's bedroom and leaves him forever changed. A rational man, the writer tries to explain away the event by blaming it on a bad dream and a fault in the newly installed security system. It is only when Whitley's house-guest Alex (Andreas Katsulas, the one-armed man in Andrew Davis' **The Fugitive**) insists he be taken home immediately that the author begins to wonder whether something strange really did take place.

Back in his New York apartment building, Strieber succumbs to a peculiar paranoia that prevents him from working and puts a strain on his marriage. A second trip to the country over the Christmas holidays is brought to an abrupt halt when a wired Whitley almost accidentally shoots his wife. Noticing a small scar on his head, he visits a doctor who informs him that he has been subjected to a rectal probe (the fact that Strieber's anal examination took place on Boxing Day still makes me smile). From the doctor's office, Strieber is sent to a psychiatrist who specialises in rape cases. It is here, through hypnosis, that the writer discovers that alien "visitors" have been observing him since his childhood and they have since turned their attention to his son. The shrink tries to get Strieber to join an encounter group made

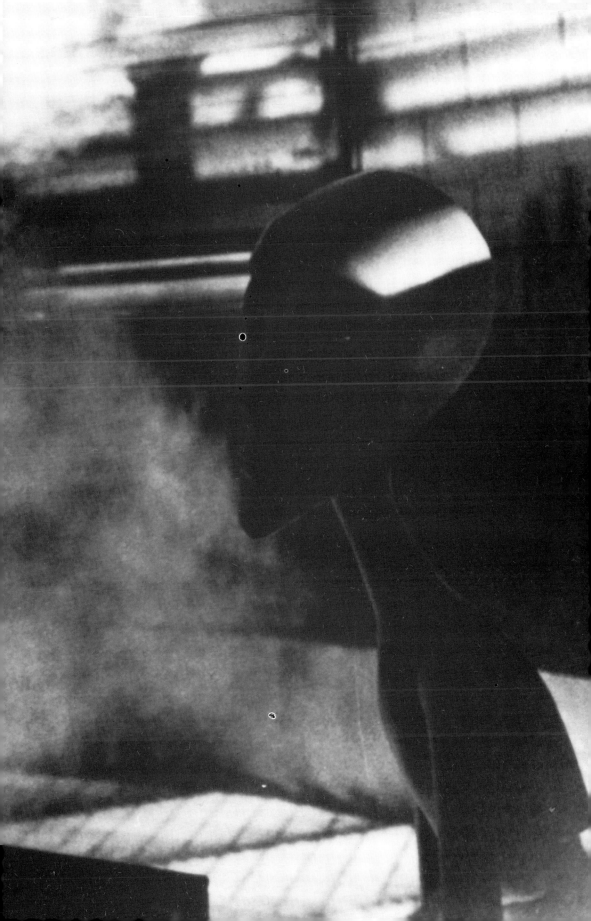

up of abductees but he refuses, choosing instead to return to his holiday home where he meets the aliens once more and undergoes his first "communion".

Strangely, it is this final fx sequence, which was clearly meant to be **Communion**'s big selling point, that is the movie's weakest element. The aliens themselves are weak rip-offs of George Lucas's jawas and the spindly creature that appears at the very end of **Close Encounters**. And while Strieber might insist that he really did kiss, high-five and dance with the aliens, the sight of Walken performing these actions on-screen is so risible as to taint the entire picture.

It's also pretty hard to get excited about the film's conclusion in which Strieber and his wife walk around a gallery debating the significance of his visitations. The problem here is that, rather like *The X-Files* with its nauseating "the truth is out there" moxy, the only truth **Communion** is capable of delivering is a fiction. It won't be until a UFO lands outside the White House or in Trafalgar Square that the world will be truly convinced of the existence of extraterrestrial life. Until such an event takes place, no amount of talk about the "visitors" representing the many faces of God will do anything to improve the reputation aliens have for being, at best, strange deviants utterly obsessed with anal probing and cattle mutilation or, at worse, complete fiction.

Far better than the finale is the kiss Strieber and his wife share just prior to it. It may not rival Bergman and Bogart on the list of "great smackers of all time", but it possesses that wonderful, world-stopping quality that all good screen kisses have. In this case, the kiss is meaningful because we know the hell these two characters have been dragged. And that we cared about these people in the first place has everything to do with Walken and the incredible Lindsay Crouse.

While Christopher Walken is the best reason to rush out and by **Communion**, it's quite obvious that his performance wouldn't be as good without his co-star. The former wife of playwright, screenwriter and director David Mamet, Crouse is rather like Walken in that she is peculiarly good at playing peculiar. Cast her as an workaday mom as Bill Forsyth did in **Being Human** and she looks completely lost. But as an uptight shrink in her ex's excellent **House Of Games**, she reveals herself to be one of the few people on earth capable of out-weirding Christopher Walken; the very reason it would seem she was cast in **Communion**.

Crouse's comfort with complexity contributes greatly to the naturalistic feel of Walken's performance. Were he acting opposite, say, Anne Archer ("Hollywood's favourite housewife"), Walken's Strieber really would look like an psychiatric case-study. But in the company of his unfathomable co-star, he comes across as quite the everyday bloke. He can still look bloody frightening, mind; the close-up of Walken waking up during the first visit could be a snapshot of the Devil waking up after a heavy night. If he can't hide his killer stare, Walken remains resolutely normal throughout **Communion**. By normal, I mean that he laughs, goofs about, argues rationally and cries; not unusual acting prerequisites, I know, but ones we very rarely see Christopher Walken perform on camera.

The laughter is particularly captivating, not because we haven't seen Walken laugh before (the menacing chuckle is one of his favourite tools) but because we haven't seen him laugh in so many different ways. Pre-coital giggles, self-conscious snickers, child-pleasing guffaws; Walken's array of laughs allows him to reveal the different facets of Strieber's personality. The goofing-around, on the other hand, is used by Walken as a means of establishing how super a parent and father Whitley is. During the Halloween party sequence, we get to see Strieber's willingness to indulge his little boy's fantasies but we also see just how convincing Christopher Walken is at conjuring up affection (in fact, Walken has to magic up all the love, fun and friendship in the father-son relationship since Joel Carlson is a pretty terrible actor). If he's good at compassion, Walken is positively miraculous when it comes to summoning up courage. Perhaps the most memorable moment in the film is the rendition of "Puttin' On The Ritz" Whitley performs for his wife before leaving for his "communion". At the first time of viewing, the song-and-dance number looks pretty strange. It's only later that you realise that as a display of bravado designed to shield the woman he loves from the awfulness that awaits him, Strieber's routine is every bit as brave as Lefty Ruggiero's final goodbye to his wife in **Donnie Brasco**. Meanwhile, Walken's performance is right up there with Al Pacino's in the quiet courage stakes.

Bravery isn't the only understated quality on show. The way Crouse and Walken argue is also very calm. There are none of the screaming fits Teri Garr and Richard Dreyfuss indulged in in **CE3K**. When Whitley acts weirdly (curling up in a ball in his study, freaking out at the Halloween bash) his wife is concerned for rather than angry with her husband. Rather like Cathy Moriarty's character in Donald Cammell's **White Of The Eye**, she loves her husband regardless of his eccentricities (I accept that fucking animals as David Keith does in Cammell's movie is more than mildly eccentric, but you can see what I'm getting at). And to prove that this affection is shared, Whitley, when his wife threatens to divorce him if he doesn't get help, checks into the psychiatrist's the very next day. Affection, incidentally, is the right word as Walken and Crouse (ironically, two of Hollywood's coldest fishes) generate between them a genuine warmth of the kind Tom Cruise and Nicole Kidman couldn't even achieve using Deep Heat.

The shrink's is, of course, where Walken's other great **Communion** acting coup takes place. In a deep trance, Strieber realises that his son has been undergoing the same routine of abductions and anal probes and immediately starts to cry. It isn't in fact the first time Walken cries in **Communion** – he also got a bit misty-eyed when he nearly shot his wife. But that first incident took place at night and you couldn't really tell if he was crying or simply had a heavy cold. Only on this second occasion, when he is sat in bright daylight, do you get to see the amazing sight it all its soggy glory. They're bloody good tears, too. But then would we expect anything less of Christopher Walken, wielder of handguns, slayer of millions, teller of quality fairy tales?

Having mastered the laughter, the fooling around, the bickering and the crying, Walken's greatest feat throughout the rest of the movie is to keep from corpsing. The psychiatrist's office is a joke, just like all movie psychiatrist's office (incidentally, if there are any shrinks reading this, if you have any patients who claim to have been abducted by UFOs, it's probably best not to clutter up your office with a number of small statues that look *exactly like the aliens they claim to have been abducted by*! Oh yes, and if you're counselling people who have suicidal tendencies, it's probably not a good idea to have a full-size painting of a man falling to his death on your wall, either). The shrink, incidentally, is played by Frances Sternhagen, a highly popular American sitcom actress and, therefore, completely ill-suited to such an earnest role.

The only thing funnier than the psychiatrist's office is her encounter group for Whitley. If you found Walken being out-weirded by Crouse unusual, the depiction of Christopher as the sanest person in a room full of people might send you round the twist. Even when surrounded by the worst sort of movie psychos, Walken manages to keep a commendably straight face. That he also maintains it throughout the snogging, Latin dancing and piss-poor puppet work of the final "communion" sequence is just a measure of how great an actor he is.

But then, as I said earlier, the film isn't about the fx. Rather it is about an epic trip taken by Christopher Walken – an incredible journey that takes the actor to places, both psychically (a children's nativity play) and emotionally (weeping for his threatened child), that we never thought we would see him visit. It's just a shame that Walken had to travel to these places in a vehicle as clapped-out as **Communion**. He deserves to have taken the voyage in a real Rolls Royce of a movie.

Communion could have taken Walken's career in a whole new direction, but it didn't. Instead, within a year of the film's release, he had essayed arguably his two most disturbed characters, the wired Frank White in Abel Ferrara's **King Of New York** and the sociopathic Robert in Paul Schrader's **The Comfort Of Strangers**. And since then, he has dealt almost exclusively in thugs, psychos and freaks. Still, if he gets old and the pension runs out, it's nice to know that Christopher Walken could always play those A. Wilford Brimley, "funny uncle" roles, even if his uncles would be more funny "peculiar" than funny "ha-ha".

Note – the above article concerns the special "director's cut" of **Communion** *that regularly airs on television and is the only version of the film available on video. Should you ever get a chance to watch the original version, I urge you to take it – you won't be missing out on any Walken and you'll be spared all those superfluous shots of salamanders.*

DEAD MAN WALKEN: 'KING OF NEW YORK'

When we first see Christopher Walken as Frank White in Abel Ferrara's **King Of New York** (1990) he is dressed in drab prison garb, his back is to the camera and he is hunched intensely over a book. The hand of an unseen guard extends into frame and rattles the cell bars with a baton. A buzzer sounds and the door clanks open. White stands and turns, yet remains in heavy silhouette. A couple of steps closer to the camera brings him menacingly into a shaft of light. We know from a hundred other prison films that this must either be White's day of freedom, or else his day of execution. Yet it is impossible to tell from the blank expression that Walken wears which fate it is that awaits him (it transpires to be both.) The emotion is certainly subtle and perfectly refined, but then for all Walken's famously psychotic performances his best acting always is.

In an almost clichéd series of shots Ferrara shows us the chains that have bound White for so long; the bars, the razor wire, the heavy metal gates. Ferrara creates the illusion of White melting through these gates and fences by framing long shots that pull focus sharply through the abstract shapes created by these seemingly impenetrable barriers. This is the first hint of the preternatural character that Walken and Ferrara are creating.

It is twilight. Outside of the prison gate awaits White's enormous, ostentatious stretched limousine, a crowning symbol of his wealth and power. Seated silently in the back of the car and accompanied by two prostitutes, White stares out of the window with the deadest of eyes. Everything is cast in an eerie electric blue light – colour coding is central to Ferrara's film, at once recalling and exaggerating the phantasmagoria of light that Scorsese created in **Mean Streets** and **Taxi Driver.** The cinematography further adds to the supernatural, spectral face of White. He falls in and out of shadow as the car sweeps past streetlights, he is living between two worlds – life, death, life, death – Walken is already establishing his character as a dead-man walking.

The journey back to the city of which he would be king has a strong sense of mythological homecoming. He rises from the steam-filled underbelly, peopled by yet more living dead – drug-addled prostitutes and hobos warming themselves around flaming trash-cans – and swoops up into the high-rise magnificence of Manhattan, Lazarus-like. Later he will simply state "I'm back from the dead". And indeed he is and back with a vengeance, but White knows that this is all borrowed time.

Whilst he takes a long, cleansing shower in his Plaza Hotel suite, savouring what must be his first moment of privacy for a long time, Ferrara

allows his camera to roam the room, falling across the clichéd symbols of wealth – the fine china, the gold trim, the champagne on ice. But none of this seems to mean much to White; the haunted, detached expression never leaves his face even when he stares directly into the camera, returning the audience's intrusive, voyeuristic gaze.

Now dressed entirely in black and standing amidst the finery of his suite, we see what is perhaps the defining image of **King Of New York**. White stands before a half-opened balcony window, the shining lights of New York projected across him. He appears to have merged, on a spiritual level, with the city he loves. To complete the picture one of the prostitutes from the limousine enters the frame and gives White his pistol, thrusting it into the top of his trousers and placing a gentle, protective hand over it.

By this point we are some 15 minutes into the film and Walken has uttered just two words, a barely audible "Thank you" to the limousine prostitute who passed him a cigarette. And yet he has already told us more about Frank White's character than a dozen pages of dialogue could have hoped to do. The simple, haunted acting style that Walken employs, in such contrast to so many of his almost self-parodying psychotic roles, is restrained and perfectly metered. It seems an irony that a director of such famed excess as Abel Ferrara should be the one to extract such a suppressed performance.

Having armed White with his pistol the woman tells him that there is someone here to see him. That someone is Jimmy Jump (Laurence Fishburne), one of White's lieutenants. We have previously seen Jump double-crossing (and executing) a Colombian drug baron, King Tito, during a drugs deal. Jump is here, along with more of White's army, to welcome him home – a welcome that is part strange machismo ritual, part high-school high-jinx. It begins with the two men facing each other down and making the following exchange:

White: "What's in the cup?"
Jump: "Rootbeer" (he crushes the paper cup) "You want some?"
White: "There's some things I don't do."

The words remain mysterious to the audience but clearly hold some deeper significance for the two men. After another perfectly timed beat, a smile begins to spread across White's face. Suddenly the whole room joins in a chant/dance, which ends with much hugging, backslapping and whooping.

From this moment in the film White is rarely alone. Those that support and protect him, either physically or legally, constantly surround him. Perhaps it would be more accurate to say that he is never without *company*, because Walken's detached performance keeps him forever *alone*, forever at arm's length from peers or true confidantes.

This scene also adds a further subtle dimension to White's character. As Jimmy Jump raps on in clichéd gangster jive, White appears to try and "fit in", almost mimicking Jump's rhythm and style. He seems a little awkward and childlike in his eagerness to please his long-lost gang. This is a conundrum indeed. We have already guessed the power of Frank White and yet here he is trying to ingratiate himself with his own foot soldiers – could it be that White genuinely just wants to be liked? Or are there more subtle motives at work?

This is one of Walken's most powerfully astute scenes in this or any other of his films. Every muscle, every line in his face switches from moment to moment between joking with his men and barking out "business" questions. At one point, having been told that Jump has killed Tito, White responds: "I must have been away too long because my feelings are dead, I feel no remorse – it's a terrible thing." With this line Walken manages to sum up both emotions simultaneously. It is, on the one hand a glib throw-away line intended to amuse his friends, whilst on the other it is probably the truest line he delivers in the film and yet another allusion to his "living dead" existence.

Ferrara's least subtle reference to Frank White's undead persona comes in a scene in which Triad gangster Larry Wong (Joey Chin) discusses details of a drugs deal with one of White's main lieutenants, whilst watching Murnau's 1922 **Nosferatu**. As the meeting concludes Wong says: "Why not stick around? I've got Frankenstein coming on next." Yet another reference not only to White's resurrected status, but possibly to the fact that White has created the mobster monster in his own image and knows that it must inevitably be destroyed. Interestingly, on a point of trivia, just two years later Walken appeared in Tim Burton's **Batman Returns** playing a character called Max Shreck – the name of the actor who portrayed the original Nosferatu.

When we see White in his "natural" habitat, an expensive New York eatery, his grace and ease of movement is mercurial. He seems to glide across the floor pressing home handshakes, greeting judges, lawyer, columnists; all toasting his release. Yet there is still a sense of unease somewhere in the background of Walken's performance. Perhaps this is the company to which he aspires but which he knows, in the depths of his dead soul, he can never truly attain. Is this reason he surrounds himself with so much finery whilst appearing to take such little joy in the luxury they provide? These things are simple props kept at hand to help him "fit in". Once again it is the chameleon-like qualities that Walken brings to the role that add these subtle depths to Frank White's persona.

As we have previously witnessed in the scene in which he addresses his foot soldiers, White is able to switch, in the blink of an eye, between characters and now in the restaurant we see the performance perfected.

White "plays to the crowd", including the previously mentioned "I'm back from the dead" remark and a quip about people like himself "...*being* the legal process". He then switches to talk business with another of his lieutenants and then switches once more to become the smooth seducer of his lawyer/girlfriend Jennifer (Janet Julian). With each change there is a barely perceptible shift in Walken's voice, a barely noticeable change in his facial expression – but it is there and it's deliberate and it's powerful.

The scene aboard a subway train in which he kisses and caresses Jennifer is a further reinforcement of two of the main persona elements already established. Firstly there is the remoteness with which White caresses his beautiful companion. Even when cupping her naked breast in his hand (it would hardly be a Ferrara film without the trademark "fleeting nipple" shot) he looks down with eyes that barely seem to register life. Secondly we again see White's desire to "belong"; this time with a gang of would-be muggers. However we now begin to truly understand how he uses this chameleon quality to his advantage. Not only does he defuse the situation (despite having asserted his superior position by letting the gang see a fleeting glimpse of his gun) he also manipulates the encounter to his advantage, turning the meeting with the gang into a recruitment opportunity for Frank White Inc.

The threat of violence that bubbles just beneath the surface of White's character has until this point been established in three ways. Firstly there is the general assumption that a character such as this has not attained such heady heights simply by being *nice* to people. The gangster genre is almost as old as cinema itself and there are rules and conventions that are readily understood by the audience. Indeed Ferrara and screenwriter Nicholas St. John are heavily influenced (on occasions not too subtly) by Howard Hawks' 1932 **Scarface**. Secondly there is the sense of danger that Walken's performance generates. A feeling that explosive violence could erupt from behind those dead eyes at any time. This is an emotion that has been created by guileful gestures and expressions in conjunction with a mixture of deadpan/dead delivery and perfectly timed dialogue. Thirdly in casting an actor such as Walken, Ferrara is able to bring a ready-made history to the character. There are inherent expectations about his screen persona that have been developed across a range of performances; from **The Deer Hunter** and **The Dogs Of War** to his maniacal performance as Max Zorin in **A View To A Kill**.

In White's confrontation with Arty Clay we see this sense of violence finally realised. Executing the old style Italian-American Mafioso in front of his own gang and in his own smokey backroom sanctuary is an act of extreme machismo. Again there is a sense of White playing to his audience, doing what is expected of him, but there is more to this execution. White doesn't merely kill Clay; he empties an entire clip into the still twitching corpse. Not only is this an "extreme killing", where White is able to re-establish his lapsed authority, there is also a sense of catharsis. This, presumably, is his first kill since going to prison and although White never seems to enjoy killing this is, at least, a return to doing what he is good at.

The bravado of killing Clay in this manner is later echoed in the drive-by execution of police officer, and Frank White nemesis, Gilley. These killings are the self-destructive acts of a man that knows he is living on borrowed time, they are the sick suicide-note that White is leaving to the city.

White's sense of borrowed time is finally vocalised in a balcony scene with Jennifer. When he expresses regret over lost time he may superficially be referring to his years spent in jail but there is a greater sense that he may mean time lost in "playing" at gangster. He tells Jennifer that he needs to "do something good" before his time is finally up but when he focuses on trying to keep open a threatened neighbourhood hospital there are strongly mixed motivations at work. Whilst the cause may at first seem noble, his methods and his meta-motives are anything but. On the one hand White organises charity drives for funds, but on the other we know that the majority of the money will be raised by his criminal activities.

Worse, these very activities – primarily drug deals – are the very thing that creates the need for such a penniless ghetto hospital. The economy of his business creates a feeding chain in which it is the poorest that suffer the most, both as a result of the drugs themselves and because of the violence that is intrinsically linked with the "industry" .

White's commitment to the cause is also further evidence of his desire to fit in with every social stratum. In keeping the hospital open he will become a hero to the local community (even if he *is* killing them with drugs), but he will also have been seen to have *achieved* something in the eyes of the city fathers – whose political agendas have tied their hands so effectively. A further self-serving motive is that he will have one up on the very same city authorities he hopes to impress with his philanthropic activities. He is, in part, achieving the mayoral ambitions that he earlier expressed.

In a scene that epitomises the hypocrisy, intentional or otherwise, of White's actions we see him escorting Wong around a ward in the hospital he intends to save. Inevitably it is a children's ward, hammering home the pity and upping the White humanitarian stakes. He even plays (a little absent-mindedly) with a child's cuddly toy, all the while discussing a huge cocaine deal with the rival gangster. Ultimately, of course, White kills Wong and simply takes the coke as if it were rightfully his.

The utter corruption of White's actions is interestingly reflected in Ferrara's 1992 **Bad Lieutenant**, in which Harvey Keitel plays the titular corrupt officer. Whilst White is basically a gangster attempting, or at least giving an illusion of attempting, to do "good", the Lieutenant is effectively his alter-ego – a police officer involved in every vice conceivable. It is also interesting to note the contrast in performances that Ferrara elicits from these two actors. Walken in **King Of New York** is, for the most part, the epitome of restraint, the violence exploding only in reactionary moments. A vivid contrast to so many of his prior performances. Whilst Keitel – all explosive energy, crying, shrieking and full of drug-fuelled energy – is also cast somewhat against type when you consider roles such as Charlie (**Mean Streets**) played against De Niro's psychotic Johnny Boy or even **Reservoir Dogs**' relatively stable Mr White compared to Michael Madsen's Mr Blonde. Ferrara seems to be commenting on the state of corruption not only at every level but also behind every mask.

The police in **King Of New York** (signalled by red lighting) are as morally ambiguous as Walken's character. Flanigan (Wesley Snipes) and Gilley (David Caruso) are effectively "bad" cops, willing to take the law into their own hands when they find their way continuously blocked by the legal

system. They are countered by "good" cop Bishop (Victor Argo – a veteran Scorsese collaborator). Bishop always tries to remain within the legal system but is clearly a physically broken man as a result of the effort that this demands.

In the penultimate scene between Bishop and White, White does his best to vocalise his own moral standpoint. Bishop, over simplistic as ever, asks him if he expects to get away with having killed so many of his rivals. White's answers: "I spent half my life in prison, I never got away with anything and I never killed anyone who didn't deserve it." This is perfectly demonstrative of his resignation to the fates, the very reason he knows he is living on borrowed time. It also shows White's ability to define his own moral corner – to decide who *deserves* to live and die. To hammer the point home Bishop demands angrily "Who made you judge and jury?" a question which recalls White's early restaurant conversation about people like him *being* the legal system. At this point, however, the question genuinely seems to throw him, Walken's brow furrows for just a second before resorting to the crowd-pleasing quip "It's a tough job but somebody has to do it."

Both Bishop and White are dressed identically in this scene and both stand almost entirely in shadow. Despite the growing similarities, in White's eyes at least, between the two men Ferrara's omnipresent colour coding still reminds us on which "side" they belong. White remains silhouetted in front of a blue-lit window, Bishop stands with his back to a door through which orange/red light spills.

White continues to lecture Bishop on the realities of his situation, desperately trying to raise his own moral position: "I'm not your problem. I'm just a business man." Knowing how empty his words must sound to Bishop, White resorts to lowering his nemesis's position by threatening to put a bounty on his head, to make him know "...what it's like to live that way". To complete the humiliation White handcuffs Bishop to a chair using his own police issue handcuffs. Now we see White stepping into the red light and leaving Bishop alone against the electric blue of the window.

The final showdown between the two men takes place back on the subway system, a traditional Mexican stand-off complete with female hostage. White is not interested in convincing Bishop that the police are as "bad" as the criminals, only that Frank White is as "good" as Bishop. He explains to his hostage, as if talking to a child: "I don't want to hurt you but I will blow you away if I have to." And turning back to Bishop he asks: "Could *you* do that?"

Both are mortally wounded in the exchange of fire that follows. Bishop falls dead, whilst White escapes the subway and emerges up into the street, echoing his arrival in New York at the start of the film. Here he is surrounded by both blue light and sudden flashes of bright red, generated by a combination of advertising neon and police car lights.

White falls into a taxi, where he waits (as he has throughout the film) to die. Perhaps the ultimate irony is that he will die sitting in grid-locked traffic. The city itself has ground to a halt, has failed him, has killed him. White dies, not with a look of defeat on his face, but one of complete resignation.

King Of New York sits perfectly at mid-point in Walken's career. His performance as Frank White is the logical conclusion of many of his previous screen incarnations, whilst it is also the starting point for so many of his subsequent roles. White is the sophisticated career criminal that has developed from the homicidal Zorin (**View To A Kill**) or Shannon (**Dogs Of War**), whilst he also shapes the mould for **True Romance's** Vincenzo Coccotti or "The man with the Plan" (**Things To Do In Denver When You're Dead**).

Walken's performance is central to the success of **King Of New York**. Without him it could easily have been dismissed as yet another blood'n'bullets gangster tale, but thanks to the genuine subtlety of his defining performance, the film refuses to be given up on so easily. It remains as perfect testimony to a great actor.

ANOTHER CROOK, ANOTHER PLANET: CHRISTOPHER WALKEN IN 'BATMAN RETURNS'

When Bruce Wayne turns up at rival Gotham City capitalist and philanthropist Max Shreck's (Christopher Walken's) costume party in Tim Burton's **Batman Returns** (1992), he is the only man who is not wearing a mask. When Selina Kyle turns up at the same party a little later on, it is clear that she doesn't appear to have grasped the concept "costume" either. It is Max's party, however, and, like a good host should, he sets the tone with a ridiculous, outsize, jewelled turban and spangly golden eye mask that neither fools, nor is intended to fool. After all, Max's mask tells the world, costumes are mere frivolous things, disguises are there to be seen through. Of course, in the film's terms, Bruce (Batman) and Selina (Catwoman) are both in costume – they have both come to the party in drag. We are not, after all, watching "Bruce Wayne Returns"; and they cast Michelle Pfeiffer strictly according to box office: as Catwoman first, Selina Kyle a distant second.

So Bruce and Selina hover in their party togs, looking distinctly uncomfortable without the reassuring grip of leather or rubber on thigh. Sadly, however, it is just not that kind of party. Max, on the other hand, is in his element, sliding up behind Bruce and whispering into his ear with camp menace: "I am the light of the city and I am its mean, twisted soul." In charmingly sinister mood, Max has no interest whatsoever in an extended conversation with Bruce – but then who would – and, when Bruce comes on like the Boy Scout, Max just as quickly slides away: "Yawn." It is a party, after all, and Max has made his point.

Named in acknowledgement of the actor Max Schreck, who played the title role of the vampire, Count Orlock, in Murnau's silent expressionist horror film, **Nosferatu**, Burton's Shreck is made up to look even paler than Walken's naturally pallid complexion. His usual shock of black hair is also teased out and dyed grey, encouraging Todd McCarthy, *Variety*'s reviewer, to observe that "...wild-maned Walken has the right comic understatement and *sang froid* as the metropolis' leading businessman, Max Shreck."[1] Indeed his skin tone and hair, habitually worn combed back in a vague tribute to Elvis (about whom Walken has apparently written two plays), are, for the actor, the two features that identify him most readily. Once asked in an interview for his "beauty secrets" Walken replied wryly: "My skin has never seen the light of day. And I have a lot of hair. That helps."[2]

Slim, dapper and delicate featured, Max is, in the terms Walken uses to describe his own, often villainous, professional persona: "...a fragile heavy."[3] As homicidal as the next cartoon villain, Max strikes with deception rather than simple brute force. Finding Selina going through his secret files he orchestrates her attempted murder by wrong footing her and by putting her off her guard. To her cost, Selina has discovered Max's scam. She has worked out that his proposed new power plant is, in the best vampiric taste, designed to be a giant capacitor to leech power from Gotham City, not to provide it with light and warmth.

"What did curiosity do to the cat?" Max asks her, menacingly. "I'm no cat," Selina replies – although she soon will be. But then we know this because we have seen the trailer and the poster and the ads in the papers. From the moment Max catches Selina in the act, we know how this scene will play out – at least in strategic, if not necessarily in tactical terms. We are relying on Walken to make its tactical resolution unnerving, unpredictable and unforgettable. "This power plant is my legacy. It's what I leave behind for Chip. Nothing must prevent that." Chip is Max's slimy son, a er... Chip off the old block, evidently. Selina grins a nervous, disingenuous grin: "...it's not like you can just kill me."

Once again, in direct narrative terms the scene is progressing with an almost audible clicking of gears. From long experience we know that the correct Hollywood response to "...its not like you can just kill me," are words to the effect of Max's next line: "Actually it's a lot like that." What keeps us in our seats throughout this basically predictable encounter, and of course this is why they cast him in the first place, is a very particular dynamic quality in Walken's much rehearsed screen villain persona. For Ian Penman, writing in *Sight And Sound*, Walken fits easily into the tradition of screen villainy:

It may be unfashionable – reverting to a measure of our art as existential truth – but you would have to say that the reason Walken pulls us in, is king of the world in some of our hearts these days, is that on some level we believe his art reflects glints of the galaxy of the private man... Walken is... like an old-time Hollywood 'type', a Lee Marvin, in whom the promise of off-screen malady and unpredictability and danger seeps through into every role, into a series of similar if not identical roles.[4]

It is Walken's calm, laconic, icily sinister delivery which cuts Selina off as effectively as if a knife had been drawn. He moves forward. In reverse shot we see her take a step back and the window behind her is revealed. Cut back to Max, and Walken's face cracks into a huge smile. It was just a joke. In poor taste, mind you, but still a joke. So then Selina grins too, because Max's smile draws her in and it draws us in along with her, because everything is going to be – and *then* Max pushes her and she flies through the glass and plunges down. As Penman writes: "Who, after all, would throw Michelle

Pfeiffer out of a window? And do it with delight? Well, Walken would."[5]

At the heart a sociopath, as are many of the more obviously crippled and costumed characters that populate Tim Burton's cinematic worlds, Walken's Max differs in as much as he wears his mask in, rather than on, his face. There is concealment there to be sure and there are lies and there is deceit, but Max takes a leaf out of Macbeth's book: his false face, not a mask, must hide what Max's false heart doth know. For Max, like any good vampire, is first and foremost a capitalist. Whether it is the labour or the blood of others that he is exploiting makes little difference, he exploits because that is the quickest route to his goal – well perhaps because he enjoys it as well. Indeed, it is this palpable sense of enjoyment that exudes both from the actor and from the characters he plays that Walken credits towards his own success. "I suppose," he says, "people enjoy watching people who enjoy their work. There's no reason to be a professional villain unless you enjoy doing it."[6]

If exploitation is his engine, Max's goal is power. When Bruce Wayne suggests Gotham City has a power surplus and does not need the proposed power station, Max replies with his typically clipped phrasing: "Power surplus? Bruce, shame on you. No such thing. One can never have too much power. If my life has a meaning, that's the meaning." Like Gotham City and like the film's underlying Superhero narrative itself, Max the vampire/Max the capitalist plays between two key frames of reference which the film develops in parallel; that is to say between mythology and modernity. The real power behind the city, Max the vampire simultaneously evokes the corrupt, if paternalistic benevolence of Tammany Hall.

At the start of the film, there is "Boss Shreck", "Gotham's own Santa Claus", up on the podium with the mayor throwing beautifully wrapped Christmas presents to the crowd: "Santa Claus?" Max replies with false modesty, "...fraid not. I'm just a poor schmo, got lucky – and sue me if I want to give some back. I only wish I could hand out more than expensive baubles. I wish I could hand out world peace and unconditional love, wrapped in a big bow." In a speech from an early draft of Daniel Waters' screenplay, Max takes time out to justify his populist approach:

MAX: Gotham has no conception of Morality, only
Celebrity. This city loves visuals. Look at
Batman. Any other city and he would be in
an institution or out there doing singing telegrams.
Here, he is a hero.[7]

In the same early screenplay draft, the Penguin sends the Ringmaster of his Red Triangle Circus Gang after Max at about this point, once more highlighting Max's status as the real "power behind the throne" in Gotham:

*RINGMASTER: We're here to kidnap the man who runs
Gotham City.
MAYOR: Oh no, please...
RINGMASTER: (laughing into headset) Did you hear that? The mayor thought
we were talking about him!*[8]

Max is the necessary counterpoint to Batman's bland, fascistic vigilantism; to Catwoman's hyper-sexualised psychosis and to the Penguin's hyperbolic freak show grotesquerie. Three of the key components of gothic fiction – sexuality, fear and disgust – are, thus, dispersed as character functions between the three oppositional characters. In the film's terms, Catwoman turns us on, the Penguin disgusts us but, even though his role is low key and he doesn't get the full horror makeover, it is Max who is there to scare. In Walken's performance, the villainy is camped up, certainly, but it is camped up in a precise, calculated and even understated sort of way:

The face that has launched a thousand metaphors is, in fact, a precision instrument perfectly designed for Walken's specialty: the Jekyll-and-Hyde switch. One minute, he's a jolly sport grinning like a groom. Then, suddenly, a mask of psychotic rage or remorseless evil.[9]

This reputation for causing fear and unease in others, this reputation for being "...the spookiest actor on film", has to a limited extent, bled over into Walken's own life.[10] Although he has, by his own admission, a pretty stable and conservative family life, Walken does worry his wife, Georgianne, on occasion. "Chris is ordinary in an unordinary way," she says of him, but admits to staying out of his way if he is working on a "dark" role.[11] He has even been known to scare himself:

*While filming Paul Schrader's **The Comfort Of Strangers** I did [scare myself]. I don't know if there are people like him, but that was a hard character to be with every day. I was glad when that one was over. I remember sitting in the dressing room outside of Rome, killing time and reading a book, and suddenly I looked up and saw myself in the mirror, and I had exactly the same reaction that I would have if I was in a restaurant and saw somebody I absolutely did not want to see. I looked up and quickly looked away, thinking, 'I hope he leaves, I hope he didn't see me'.*[12]

And yet Walken's schtick is not just scary, he works because he does scary-funny to perfection. He plays Macbeth and the Porter, both in one

body; he plays the villain and the comic relief that paces tragedy and gothic alike. An actor who is serious about his career and his craft, he is also in healthy touch with the absurdity of some of his roles, in particular his work in **Batman Returns** which he acknowledges was "over the top" and in the James Bond film **A View To A Kill**:

In the Bond film I had my hair dyed an impossible yellow color, and that became my motivation in a lot of the scenes: I had a secret subtext, which I never discussed with anybody. Every time I had a scene with somebody I'd be thinking: 'What do you think of my hair? Do you like my hair? Do you like what they did to me? That they made me look like this?' So next time you see the movie, every time I torture somebody I'm really thinking: 'You see what they did to me with this hair?'[13]

Although he laughs off his performance in **Batman Returns** as just a part in a "costume movie", Walken clearly admires Tim Burton and tells this story as an example of what makes Burton his kind of director:

At the beginning of the shoot I was standing with him, waiting for them to light the set, and I said that in The Great Gatsby, Gatsby and Nick Carraway are having lunch with the gangster Meyer Wolfsheim, and Nick notices that Wolfsheim is wearing cuff links made out of human molars. Burton calls over his assistant and says, 'Get him cuff links made out of human molars.' Within half an hour the guy comes back with them, and I wore them throughout the

movie. It's something the audience wouldn't know, but Burton knew it would be good for me to have them.[14]

Walken has often appeared reluctant to discuss his work in terms of craft. For him, the acting process is just not something good actors discuss, and certainly not amongst themselves:

The last thing good actors talk about is acting... Actors share an unspoken language. They may be going after different angles, but they're focused on the same thing, which is making the scene work.[15]

When Walken does discuss his craft, the metaphors that come to him for the truth of what he does are drawn both from fine art and physics:

If there were different acting schools, as there are different schools of painting, I think I'd be an abstract actor. I look at my subject in a fragmented way, and when I do see the truth about something it's obliquely, by feeling more than reason.[16]

There are different kinds of energies. My energy is a kind of implosion. I think I've always been that way – it's one of my qualities. The point is that someone with the capacity for implosion also has the capacity to explode.[17]

This sense of understatement, this sense of the containment of overpowering energies just below the surface of a role, has become the easy trademark by which journalists and critics (like *Variety*'s Todd McCarthy) have in their turn approached their own definitions of Walken's star quality. Many of what one might call the signature moments of his acting career have turned on just this kind of passionate reserve. Examples are too numerous to list, but would include the showdown with his brother's killer in Abel Ferrara's **The Funeral**; the interrogation scene with Dennis Hopper in **True Romance** and, of course, in the role that made his name as a film actor, the final game of Russian Roulette in **The Deer Hunter**. Even in the "costume movie" **Batman Returns** there is his exit line, his brief, doomed attempt to bargain for his life with Catwoman, which fits this same pattern. What can Max bribe her with to spare him, "...money, jewels, a very big ball of string?" We accept this humour at the moment of death because this is an action movie and we understand the genre's conventions but, more importantly, because we have come to accept Walken's eccentric performance style not just as relief from the "gothic effect" stuffiness of the Batman's characterisation but as an important attraction in itself:

I've always been a little exotic – that's the truth – but mostly for one basic reason: I've been in show business since I was a year old. I grew up with gypsies and singers and dancers running around me – that is the planet I come from. The language I use, the way I express myself, it all comes from there. When I was ten years old, I was working with Jerry Lewis.[18]

Walken sees himself as a quiet person, an introvert. He doesn't enjoy parties, stands around like a wallflower, rarely says much unless he is talking to friends. This quietness comes through in his screen acting, but he sees himself differently when he is on stage:

There's an expression with actors that less is more. Sometimes that works. On the other hand there are great actors who don't go by that principle at all. Where would Laurence Olivier be with less is more? Or Groucho Marx for that matter? I think I have a natural tendency to watch. That's what I do best... An observer is not a bad thing for an actor to be... Actually, I've been criticized for not being inhibited enough onstage. Here I tend to be extrovert, but not in the movies. I wish I were more of an extrovert in the movies – I might get different kinds of parts.[19]

As we have already seen, Max Shreck, when he does speak, speaks in short, clipped phrases. In as much as he is a sort of anal extrovert, a passionate retentive, Max is a classic Walken character. It is as if he is speaking his own shorthand, as if expansive language would let too much out, give too much away. And yet within the constricted boundaries of his speech, there is room for more humour and more – albeit perverse – emotional commitment than Batman the hero ever proves capable of. This retentive approach to conversation is admirably illustrated after he is kidnapped by the Penguin who accuses him of being a monster. Full of *sang froid*, Max replies: "Frankly I feel it's a bum rap. I'm a business man. Tough, yes. Shrewd, OK. But that does not make me a monster." Ironically, for such an anal man, it is his polluted evacuations that have given him away. The sewer-dwelling Penguin, who has swum in Max's toxic waste and who has pasted together the shredded evidence of Max's schemes, knows the truth: "Don't embarrass yourself, Max. I know all about you. What you hide, I discover. What you put in your toilet, I put on my mantle. Get the picture?"

Like Bruce and Selina in their own ways, the Penguin does not see through the mask that is Max's face when it is presented to him. No, Max tricks, manipulates and betrays his erstwhile partner as easily as look him in the eye. The Penguin sees only the truth of what ends up in his world, the monstrous world, the world of disgust. Catwoman sees through Max's mask well enough, but it took her own blindness, death and subsequent re-birth as the expression of all Selina's repression to do it. Bruce doesn't like Max, but he can't see the truth either because his vision is blinkered by the eyeholes of the Batman's cowl. But then poor damaged Bruce needs to be a little naive in order for us to forgive the violence that attends his eventual awakening to the truth.

In a film which, if it is about anything, is about the power of deception, Max is there to teach Gotham City the lesson it never seems to learn. Max is there to teach Gotham finally to start to "think gothic", to see the skull beneath the skin before the Bat Signal has to play upon the clouds; before the body count begins to rise once again. The fact that his lesson is triumphantly forgotten in a succession of increasingly poor sequels is testament to the power of an altogether more impressive kind of vampire than Max can ever aspire to become. The fact that it is Christopher Walken, the quiet man, the family man, who is contracted in as the supply teacher may have something to do with his understated, well balanced approach to moments of social tension:

The other day we had a driver who was a young, good-looking guy. He was talking to [my wife] and I thought he was a little cocky and flirty. I found myself staring at him, like, 'Kid, should I eat you from your toes or from your nose?'[20]

NOTES

1. Todd McCarthy, "Batman Returns", *Variety* June 15th, 1992.

2. Steven Garbarino, "Christopher Walken", *Interview* Vol.23 #7, July 1993 p.72.

3. Ibid. p.72.

4. Ian Penman, "The Dead Christopher Walken", *Sight And Sound* Vol.7 #1, January 1997. p.7. Incidentally, an early draft of Daniel Waters' screenplay for **Batman Returns** has Selina returning to the office just as Max and Chip had finished planning the Penguin's crime spree as a catalyst for the Penguin's mayoral election campaign. In this draft, Selina is killed because Max is worried that she may have overheard. She is still pushed out of the window, and the dialogue immediately leading up to the event is very similar.

5. Ibid. p.7.

6. Garbarino: 1993, p.71.

7. Daniel Waters, **Batman Returns** (early screenplay draft), www.lontano.org/FMA/arkiv/batman-returns.html.

8. Ibid.

9. Michael Kurcfeld, "The Mr. Showbiz Interview: Christopher Walken", mrshowbiz.go.com /interviews/409_1.html, 1999.

10. Lawrence Grobel, *Playboy* interview: Christopher Walken www.geocities.com/Hollywood/Theater/4298/playboy. html, 1997.

11. Garbarino: 1993, p.71.

12. Ibid. p.7.

13. Grobel: 1997.

14. Ibid.

15. Garbarino: 1993, p.72.

16. Chuck Pfeifer & Mark Matousek, "In The Danger Zone", *Interview* Vol.18 #3 March, 1988.

17. Garbarino: 1993, p.72.

18. Ibid. p.72.

19. Pfeifer & Matousek: 1988, p.76.

20. Grobel: 1997.

HEAVEN MUST BE MISSING AN ANGEL: 'THE PROPHECY'

The Prophecy (1995) is a rare and blessed thing, a dumb movie that makes its audience feel smart. As such, it's part of a small but entertaining sub-genre, dominated by horror but also featuring contributions from historical dramas, science fiction flicks and thrillers. The ploy on the part of the film-makers is a simple one – to give their material some semblance of intellectual depth and cultural resonance by kitting it out with references to history, literature or, of course, the bible.

Think of modern takes on the vampire myth: whether tongue in cheek (*Buffy*, **Sundown, The Lost Boys**) or deadly serious (**The Addiction**, TV's superlative *Ultraviolet*), all have relied on the viewer's awareness of bloodsucking folklore and fictions. The characters depicted exist in a world culturally familiar with vampires, so it's necessary for the film-maker to either exploit or reverse our expectations. (It's an approach Kevin Williamson took to its logical conclusion when reinventing the slasher movie with his screenplay for **Scream** – more on that film later.) Think of the last time you saw a sci-fi movie that wasn't buckling under the weight of its own allegorical pretensions. Think of **Seven**, which went so far as to feature a hero who was slower than the audience in spotting the literary precedents for the homicides under investigation. However it's horror – particularly demonic/satanic horror – which goes one step further, actually utilising the Bible as freely adaptable source material, so much so that the early evangelists could probably demand an "original story" credit.

Rosemary's Baby and **The Exorcist** paved the way with their depictions of demonic violation and possession, although Polanski's film was strangely secular, or perhaps even pagan in its attitude to the forces of evil. Rosemary's neighbours were devotees of the black arts, practitioners of witchcraft revelling in their own gifts rather than seeking to bring about the apocalypse. William Friedkin and novelist/screenwriter William Peter Blatty upped the spiritual ante by involving catholic priests in their story. The film's success can be attributed to this decision to treat the concept of an immortal soul with gravity – in so doing, it made the audience fear for their own. The message of **The Exorcist** can be read as this: the devil exists, and he wants you. The message of **The Omen** movies, on the other hand, is that the devil exists and he wants all of us.

Chronicling the life and work of Damien Thorn is as blatant as the cinema gets in exploiting the good book. What schoolkid didn't go scurrying for the nearest bible immediately after seeing the Satanic trilogy? None of us were disappointed – it was all there in the *Book Of Revelation*: the beast, the angel isle, the Anti-Christ, 666. The movies, already pretty scary on superficial terms (David Warner's decapitation, Billie Whitelaw, the music, the whole Rottweiler thing), suddenly took on greater weight than their artistic qualities deserved. They drew on collective unconsciousness, folk memory and the depth charges planted by primary school religious education, and blurred the line between cinematic fiction and "fact". For an entire generation **The Omen** represented our first taste of a modern horror movie (the TV première of the first film drew enormous ratings in the UK, just before the home video boom of the mid-'80s meant that kids could get their hands on all the terror they were ever going to need). It gave us a taste for spiritual horror which was partly fed by the likes of **Angel Heart**, but was never truly satisfied until **The Prophecy** came along. **The Prophecy** was an absolute godsend.

THE WAR IN HEAVEN

Gregory Widen's film has everything thing the pseudo-religious, intellectually insecure gore hound could possibly want – biblical origins, visual jokes based on gothic architecture, catholic imagery and (always a favourite) stuff in Latin. Beneath this elaborate window-dressing lies a relatively simple story: a young would-be priest (Thomas, as in Doubting) loses his faith at the very moment of ordination when he experiences horrendous visions of angels committing atrocities upon each other. Years later Thomas, now a homicide detective, is visited in his New York apartment by an angel called Simon (as with all the other angels in the film, Simon is first glimpsed perched on a ledge, as if looking down from Notre Dame cathedral). This heavenly messenger assures Thomas that he is part of God's plan, before leaving the cop alone to struggle with what exactly this means. Simon then receives a visitor of his own who is far less friendly: he and this hostile angel fight to the death, and Simon escapes to Arizona. Thomas is assigned the murder investigation, largely because Simon had left a copy of the former seminarian's thesis on the nature of God's relationship with man and the angels at the scene of the crime.

The autopsy reveals that the victim had no eyes or optical tissue of any kind, and had the genetic profile of an aborted foetus. His only possession is an ancient bible, bookmarked at the 23rd Chapter of the *Book Of Revelation* – this captures Thomas' attention immediately, since there *is* no 23rd Chapter. As he translates the chapter, he learns of a Second War in Heaven. The first war had occurred when Lucifer got ideas above his station and had to be kicked downstairs, but the second had its roots in God's treatment of man: when Jesus became man, he made man the equal of God and therefore superior to angels. A disgruntled faction took umbrage at this

and, lead by former favourite Gabriel, rebelled against God. As Thomas reads this, Gabriel himself (Christopher Walken) visits the morgue to give his fallen comrade a fiery send-off.

The action then switches to Arizona where Simon steals the soul of a dead army general who had committed atrocities in Korea. It's this soul Gabriel wants for its ferocity and military acumen. Simon hides it in the living body of a young Native American girl, Mary, before being killed by Gabriel. Gabriel then talks to the local school children (winning them over with impromptu trumpet lessons) and learns of the girl's whereabouts – he must kill her to retrieve the soul. Thomas is in town by now too, and the stage is set for a dramatic final confrontation. In the desert, Mary's family seek to purge her of the evil spirit, but Gabriel arrives mid-ceremony. All seems lost until Lucifer himself intervenes, killing Gabriel and eating his heart – the devil doesn't need the competition of another bad angel. Order is restored in heaven, hell, and on earth.

HIP TO BE SCARED

The Prophecy was produced by Dimension Films, a spin-off of the independent giant, Miramax. Dimension chairman Bob Weinstein was looking to create a credible modern horror movie, which may not sound like too great a task, but in pre-**Blair Witch/Sixth Sense** Hollywood was positively gargantuan. Weinstein decided to follow his indie instincts and give a writer a shot at directing his own screenplay.[1] Gregory Widen's most significant credit to that point had been for original story on the first **Highlander** movie, but Dimension gave him his head. A half-decent budget and the production company's Miramax-based clout helped Widen attract a hipper cast than the genre was used to at that point. Elias Koteas (Thomas) may have earned a crust early in his career thanks to the Teenage Mutant Ninja Turtles, but he was also the actor of choice for art house darling Atom Egoyan. Viggo Mortensen was an acknowledged Method tough guy, noted for his sleazy turns in **Carlito's Way** and Sean Penn's **Indian Runner**. Eric Stoltz (Simon) and Amanda Plummer were still surfing the post-**Pulp Fiction** wave of indie cred. Receiving top billing however, was another cameo performer from Tarantino's urban instant classic – Christopher Walken.

ENTERTAINING ANGEL

Even within the context of Walken's career to date, his performance in **The Prophecy** is a strange one. While Stoltz, Mortensen and especially Koteas play every scene straight as though their immortal soul depended upon it, Walken's tongue is most often found in his cheek: when it's not licking furniture for traces of angel blood, that is. Thus Thomas can ruminate aloud: "Did you ever notice how in the Bible, when ever God needed to punish someone, or make an example, or whenever God needed a killing, he sent an angel? Did you ever wonder what a creature like that must be like? A whole existence spent praising your God, but always with one wing dipped in blood. Would you ever really want to see an angel?"

While Gabriel is far less keen on human moral philosophy: "I'm an angel. I kill newborns while their mamas watch. I turn cities into salt. And occasionally, when I feel like it, I tear little girls apart. And from now till kingdom come... the only thing you can count on... in your existence... is never understanding why."

Gabriel also gets to deliver the best gags, sarcastically telling a group of grade schoolers: "Study your math, kids. Key to the Universe."

When, later, the same class' teacher tells him to "go to hell," he utters the snappy comeback: "Heaven, heaven. At least get the zip code right."

As well as these humorous asides and over the top, action movie villain moments, there's the entire question of Gabriel's relationship with Jerry to consider. Jerry is a half-successful suicide, slowly decaying but kept alive by Gabriel to act as a slave and earthly guide – a driving licence not being among his angelic gifts. They are a kind of Prospero and Ariel in reverse, with Gabriel fine when it comes to magic, but hopeless in more mundane matters. Walken and Adam Goldberg play their scenes together like a comedy double act, with the older actor's serene and imperious put-downs working in contrast to the younger man's constant whining. Entertaining these sequences – and by extension Walken's performance as a whole – may be, but are they out of place in a film which is supposed to address such complex issues as God's relationship to man and the nature of faith? On the surface, Walken's dialogue and delivery do seem to detract from the film's portentous themes, but closer inspection reveals a perfectly cast actor doing spectacular justice to a tailor-made role.

The two key elements to Gabriel's character are pride and contempt. He is proud of his own race, of the gifts he possesses as an angel, of state of grace he enjoyed after doing God's will with such obedience and flair. His contempt is reserved for another race – humans. He cannot believe that the species he constantly refers to as "talking monkeys" could have been promoted above angels in the universal hierarchy.

Since these are his character's twin motivations, it is entirely natural that Walken should stomp through the film, preening himself whenever possible, spitting forth bile whenever he comes across a human. Gabriel clearly feels his acts are beyond the comprehension of mankind, and so wastes no time attempting to explain himself. It's here that the casting of Walken is so important: such is his iconic stature, especially among the indie kids populating the film, that much of his character work is done before he opens his mouth. Walken the actor is not someone to be judged by conventions, much as Gabriel the character considers himself as part of a higher state of being. Of note also is his name above the title top billing. Elias Koteas is clearly the film's leading man, but Walken is undoubtedly its star. And Walken obviously enjoyed the role – he reprised it in **Prophecy II** (1998), and will reportedly return again in **Prophecy III** in (appropriately) the year 2000.

JESUS LOVES YOU
For a box office failure which went straight to video in Britain, **The Prophecy** has some unlikely admirers, chiefly the contributors to the Hollywood Jesus website. This site is dedicated to finding the word of god hidden in the recesses of Hollywood's unholy output, and it absolutely adores **The Prophecy**. For dedicated Christians, the film's affirmation of the importance of faith, of the strength of God's relationship with man, far outweighs the

blasphemous implications of depicting angels as megalomaniac psychotics. Indeed, Hollywood Jesus head honcho David Bruce goes out of his way to mount a biblical defence of the film: "The Bible tells us that there is a spiritual war going on right now, it says, 'For we are not fighting against people made of flesh and blood, but against the evil rulers and authorities of the unseen world, against those mighty powers of darkness who rule this world, and against wicked spirits in the heavenly realms' (Ephes. 6:12 NLT). This film gives us a fictional peek of this war in the heavenly realms."

Note the use of the term "fictional" – we won't get to see the real thing until the last day. Bruce also finds character motivation in the pages of the good book: "...humans have been brought into glory because of the death of Christ (Hebrews 2:10-11) and humans will judge angels as the Bible says (1 Cor. 6:3). This is the biblical basis for the jealousy of the angels toward humans in the film. '...Because thine heart *is* lifted up, and thou hast said, I *am* a God, I sit *in* the seat of God... thou set thine heart as the heart of God' (Ezekiel 28:2 KJV)"

Reading such stuff, one can't help but reassess Widen's motives in making in the film. Did he set out to make a classy, apocalyptic horror movie or was he intent on provoking theological debate? In an ever more atheistic (or at least agnostic) Europe, this may seem a strange question, yet in the still God-fearing USA the situation is more complex. For many Americans like David Bruce, the world of **The Prophecy** requires very little suspension of disbelief – it is the world they inhabit, much as watching a contemporary urban drama takes place in the world the rest of us inhabit. Is Widen conscious of that? It might explain the absence of any post modern reactions within the screenplay – at no point does anyone question the existence of God, Satan or angels.

To what extent does Widen share Christian beliefs? Is he attempting to spread the word in some way? Almost certainly not, but when one considers that **The Exorcist** was slammed in certain quarters as a recruitment drive for the Catholic Church, it's hard to watch a far less complex film like **The Prophecy** without thinking of its propaganda possibilities. It's worth watching the movie again, alongside Michael Tolkin's fantastic directorial debut **The Rapture** (1991): that film went the whole hog and staged the ending of the world, yet was all the more compelling for being set among initially cynical, sinful non-believers. (**The Rapture** may be one of the great lost films of the past ten years. Tolkin made his name with the screenplay for **The Player**, but **The Rapture** is superior to Altman's limp satire in every respect.)

Whether we view **The Prophecy** as Christian dogma, above average horror, or the spiritual heir to **The Omen** and **The Exorcist**, there is no doubting its greatest asset. Christopher Walken may be the only actor alive who possessed the qualities of otherworldly strangeness and in-your-face menace essential to the portrayal of an avenging angel – think how bad other actors have been when portraying heavenly messengers (Nicholas Cage, you know who you are). The sheer Walkenesque nature of this role, this performance, makes it worthy of inclusion in any appreciation of the actor's work to date, confirming as it does what we've known for years: there's no one on earth like him.

NOTES

1. Dimension were almost rewarded: **The Prophecy** debuted at number one in the US box office charts, before plummeting like a stone. It never received a cinema release in Britain. Bob Weinstein learned from the experience, giving the next horror script that came his way to a genre hack, and casting a host of drop-dead gorgeous young television stars instead of art house regulars. The script was called "Scary Movie", but had its title changed to **Scream**. Like **The Prophecy**, it has two inferior sequels: unlike **The Prophecy** it was an international smash hit and cultural phenomenon. Gregory Widen should've cracked jokes about **The Omen** and **The Exorcist**, but who knew?

SHOOTING UP ON SPEECH: THE FEMALE "FIX" OF 'THE ADDICTION'

Body fluids attest to the permeability of the body, its necessary dependence on an outside, its liability to collapse into this outside (this is what death implies), to the perilous divisions between the bodies inside and outside. They affront a subject's aspiration toward autonomy and self-identity. They attest to a certain irreducible "dirt" or disgust, a horror of the unknown or the unspecifiable that permeates, lurks, lingers and at times leaks out of the body, a testimony of the fraudulence or impossibility of the "clean" and "proper".[1]

INTRODUCTION

On first appearance it may seem odd to choose **The Addiction** (1995) for a volume dedicated to the work of Christopher Walken. The narrative, which deals with a philosophy graduate's incorporation into a vampire cult makes a series of connections between the blood lusts of the undead and the junkie's obsession for the "fix". Rather than occupying a permanent presence within the proceedings, **The Addiction** sees Walken literally walking through his role: he is on-screen for less than fifteen minutes, being introduced as the vampire Peina towards the end of the narrative.

The film punctuates the actor's brief role with not only "stock vampire movie images" of blood and infection but also documentary footage of war deaths, civilian mutilation and holocaust memorabilia. Although the movie begins considering a female protagonist's quest for knowledge on the issues of morality and the human capacity for evil, it ends on a far more ironic and cynical note. Here, the heroine Kathleen (Lilli Taylor) and her undead entourage devour the academic members of the faculty that have just graded her doctoral thesis!

Because the choice of film purposely eschews works in which Christopher Walken takes a more prominent role, I immediately feel the need to defend my analysis of **The Addiction** over other examples from the actor's repertoire. I could hastily draw on the fact that the film does feature the star working with Abel Ferrara, one of contemporary American cinema's most challenging and consistently innovative underground directors. However, this stance would then merely open me up to the criticism that (as with the worst excesses of auteur theory) I am collapsing the importance of the actor's skills into presumptions surrounding the director's creative role.[2]

Alongside this criticism, **The Addiction** still appears to be a "bad fix" when compared to other Walken/Ferrara collaborations. Whereas the pair's powerful realisation of the redemptive aspects of the criminal code contained in **The King Of New York** (1990) ensured wholly positive reviews,[3] critical reaction to **The Addiction** was at best mixed. Although writers such as Gavin Smith praised the complex nature of the film's construction and style,[4] the narrative's continual shift from scenes of excess "necking" to narrations on Nietzsche frequently lead to claims that it was both pretentious and greatly distilled its reading of European philosophy.[5]

Even Ferrara's **The Funeral** (1996) which was released in the same period as **The Addiction** (and to a far more positive reception) would also seemingly provide a more detailed exploration of Christopher Walken's acting style, gestures and modes of performance and display. Here, he takes centre stage as Ray, the contemplative and yet corrupt head of an Italian family out to avenge what he believes is a gang-orchestrated killing of his brother.

However, rather than view **The Addiction** as an aberration to the related debates of the "Movie Top Ten" Series, I would argue the film does raise a number of interesting questions about the relationship of male acting style to wider debates around sexuality, bodily "excess" and representations of the self in language. This is because those theoretical accounts seeking to "rescue" the performer's import from an over-evaluation of the director's creative input have frequently stressed the link between the theatrical and wider social, cultural and psychological processes. For instance, certain accounts of contemporary acting style have turned to anthropology to comprehend the link between the facial gestures and contortions of folk performance and styles of accentuated acting in industrialised society.[6]

In terms of understanding the mental processes binding the performer to his or her audience, the importance of psychoanalysis to the debate around acting style has been two-fold. Firstly, certain critics have noted that the fascination audience and fan groups hold for their star object exceeds mere idealisation, pointing instead to the "psychic economy of the spectator's pleasure".[7] Using this perspective has allowed a consideration of the way in which adult sexual identity is often seen as "lacking" and incomplete, while identification with the star object offers an illusory sense of completeness to the viewer.

DISHING THE "DIRT" ON DISCOURSE: WHY BINARY OPPOSITIONS DISGUST VAMPIRES!

Beyond issues of identification, psychoanalytically informed performance theory has also facilitated an understanding of how the differences in male and female representation can be linked to issues of language and ideology. Of particular importance here is the work of the French psychoanalyst Julia

Kristeva. Via her concept of the "semiotic" bond between mother and infant, Kristeva has outlined a period of "archaic communication" existing at the earliest stages of the child's life.[8] These drives and affiliations (as well as the libidinal forces underpinning them) are repressed once the individual enters the language system.

It is this "symbolic" domain, with its emphasis on the clinical division of sexual identity through the binary polarities of speech, which Kristeva sees as working to limit the power and autonomy of the body (and in particular the female body which connotes the repressed association to the mother). However, she argues that certain unregulated and chaotic modes artistic expression threaten to evoke this repressed maternal bond both through a preoccupation with "disgusting" (infantile) bodily acts as well through the subversion of "adult" systems of communication such as rule-bound language.

Importantly, dance and theatrical performance are two such creative endeavours where physiological display frequently mimics the uncoordinated gestures of infancy. These artistic forms also point to a pattern of representations which remain difficult to articulate within established discourse. According to Elin Diamond, it is within the domain of contemporary theatre practice that Kristeva's work on the creative as semiotic finds expression. In her analysis of "The Shudder Of Catharsis", Diamond references the work of postmodern performance artist Karen Finley as emulating the uncontrollable gestures and urges of infancy. Describing her work as the embodiment of social and gender rages, Diamond notes how Finley frequently contorts her body with a series of judders and spasms, mimicking the child's inability to fully master its own physiology.

In works such as these, acting and physical performance are used to "arouse and harmonise the impure desires of the "mind's other", the passionate corporeal, sexual body".[9] Indeed, as with other forms of creativity, theatre and dance remain forms whose movements are physical and gestural, thus requiring their own specific codes of interpretation outside of the confines of established language.

If, as Kristeva argues, it is possible for the repressed semiotic bond to exist with the creative domain, then it is these infantile and archaic drives which are furnished by **The Addiction**. By virtue of its status as "vampire movie", the narrative immediately connotes the infantile world through its generic preoccupation with body fluids such as blood. However, in direct opposition to the continued Hollywood trend of depicting the vampire's activities in "exotic" or aesthetic terms, Ferrara's film emphasises the savage and disgusting process of blood extraction. As Roger Ebert commented in his review of the film "If there really were vampires, one imagines they would be more like the figures in **The Addiction**... In Abel Ferrara's film the vampires are more like rapists than like children of the night, and they need blood in much the same way that a drug addict needs a hit."[10]

From the moment where Kathleen is dragged into a garbage strewn alley and infected by another female vampire, to the climactic scene where she herself orchestrates the near-cannibalistic annihilation of her University tutors, the film makes clear that when wounded, the human body suffers and bleeds. In so doing, **The Addiction** highlights the corporeal self (and its fluids) as potential sources of social and cultural disgust.[11] This is underscored by Ferrara's frequent juxtaposition of the (fictionalised) bodies of Kathleen's victims and the real-life footage of civilian war casualties and concentration camp inmates.[12]

By focusing on the body as a site of horror, the film draws parity with Kristeva's work on cultural constructions of "dirt" and disgust. By using the term "abjection", Kristeva traces the taboos surrounding bodily matter and associated substances such as vomit, shit, spittle and (significantly) blood back to the semiotic bond between mother and child.[13] She argues that these products provoke disgust not because they contain any elements that are intrinsically harmful or distasteful, but rather because they point back to a primitive infantile period which the symbolic then seeks to repress.

It is not merely that these body fluids reference the child's obsession with exploring waste and body matter, but rather that these products are an affront to the very distinctions language uses to define and limit human identity. As Elizabeth Grosz has argued in the book *Volatile Bodies*:

The abject is what of the body falls away from it while remaining irreducible to the subject/object and inside/outside oppositions. The abject necessarily partakes of both polarised terms but cannot be clearly identified with either.[14]

Grosz (here following Kristeva) defines the abject as that which refuses to respect the borders of speech. In so doing, she points to the centrality of binary oppositions and "boundary markers" as mechanisms through which language ensures a clean cut division between the sexes (man versus woman, penis versus vagina etc). However, it is the very basis of these borders and polarities which the "dirt" of the body and its substances threatens to upturn. For instance, the blood of **The Addiction** does not merely flow, it spreads and congeals on the exterior of the skin surface, thus altering the outer body image and collapsing its distinction into the corporeal interior.[15]

This effect is most clearly marked in the vampire orgy which Kathleen orchestrates in the film's finale. As with the insatiable oral appetites of the infant, the vampires gorge themselves on the blood and flesh of their "intellectual" victims. Such is the extent of their feeding frenzy that Taylor's appearance becomes remodelled through the mass of pus and gore which remains stuck to her face following the meal.[16] In this sense, the blood of **The Addiction** taints, stains and refuses to leave the bodies and compulsions of either victim or vampire. In the words of Elizabeth Grosz, these are body fluids which are "... engulfing, difficult to be rid off;... they seep, they infiltrate; their control is a matter of vigilance, never guaranteed."[17] Furthermore, in its disrespect for the socially sanctioned boundaries of the body, waste matter and bodily fluids also come to signify the destruction of wider cultural and social boundaries within the fictional space. Indeed, reviews of the film were quick to note its depiction of the urban landscape as a sphere of social "dirt" already suffering infection. As Rob White commented, **The Addiction** is:

*... photographed in stark black and white, and the... effects look clinical, forbidding and severe. The camera tries to sanitise and cordon off the action. The images of New York are drained of both literal and human colour, and so seem anaemic and starved of air. It's as if the film makers are flinching away from the inner city streets... they conjure up, a distaste which permeates **The Addiction**.*[18]

Reiterating the theme of eroded physiological and social boundaries, it is significant that the vampire's presence also violates taboos surrounding sexual, racial and geographical distinctions. For instance, it is noticeable that Kathleen's addiction repeatedly leads her to inhabit the "black" quarters of the city; a locale where her racial difference is frequently commented upon. A point of comparison is indicated during the film's finale. Here, the heroine invites the black ghetto dwellers she has infected to feed off the white intellectuals at her graduation party.

However, it is not merely that the heroine's presence in an otherwise racially divided space violates the boundary which separates "white" from "black" culture. Rather, it is noticeable that the vampire also upturns "border" distinctions separating male and female gender identity. Indeed, it is interesting that Kathleen is infected by the androgynous figure of "Casanova" (Annabella Sciorra), whose name carries a series of male connotations, yet who appears to be gendered female. However, even these markers of sexual difference are blurred. Although Casanova appears dressed (incongruously for her ghetto setting) in black ball-gown, these signifiers of femininity jar against other features of her appearance such as her boyish haircut and the distinctly masculine display of strength with which she drags Kathleen into the alley to assault her.[19]

INFANTILE ECHOES: THE FEMALE "VOICE" OF 'THE ADDICTION'

Ultimately, it is not merely the boundary separating interior and exterior sections of the body that **The Addiction** traverses. Nor is it the fact that distinctions separating "white" from "black" culture or masculine from feminine identity are undercut by the film. Rather, Kathleen's journey through vampirism actually reverses the boundary separating the body (as a source of disgust) from the "word" (as a "pure" means of expression). Kathleen's "addiction" places her within the realm of the flesh and in this respect secures her revulsion at the processes of signification.

This reduction of the word to abject status is underscored in the restaurant scene where the heroine attempts to re-adjust to normal society following her infection. However, after meeting her friend in a diner, she becomes nauseous at this companion's insistence on eating a burger and reading philosophical text books at the same time. Rather than the dead meat being a source of disgust, it is the signifier which now offends! This reduction of language to the repulsive is also indicated in Kathleen's philosophy classes which now reduce her to fits of vomiting, as well as her definition of the college library as a locale governed by "a stench worse than a slaughterhouse".

Thus it can be seen that as infection takes hold, Kathleen increasingly withdraws from the otherwise male dominated arena of logic and discourse that the film represents. Indeed, the narrative is marked by an opposition between two types of communication. The first is the conventional "masculine" discourse or a (literal) excess of "talk" and explanation aimed at Kathleen by depicted male characters. From her lascivious college Professor (who complains that she has not "said a word all evening" when trying to seduce her), to cops and physicians attempting to verbalise what has happened to her, the film makes clear the heroine's incomparability with the sphere of male talk. As a result, it counterbalances this masculine domain with a second language, which can be seen as the beginnings of a female discourse. Although present at the margins of the narrative, this female speech remains unintelligible within the confines of conventional language use.

For instance, the film's opening sequence depicts Kathleen attending a slide display on American atrocities in Vietnam. Here the film establishes a link between grotesque physiological display and this female "voice" struggling for expression. This is intimated in Ferrara's juxtaposition of documentary footage of violated Vietnam corpses alongside the voice-over of a female child singing on the soundtrack. Although this vocal presence (which remains unintelligible from a conventional English perspective) is partially obliterated by the sudden introduction of a male voice-over claiming to "explain" the images, it remains audible as background "noise" during the scene.

This vocal presence initiates a pattern whereby infantile and female voices can frequently be heard on the soundtrack to accompany the various official spaces (such as hospitals) which attempt to cure Kathleen of her addiction. Importantly, the narrative's rejection of the binary structure of "male" language is also indicated in the heroine's literal refusal to communicate within established patterns of discourse. As a result, monologue replaces dialogue, with more space given to the heroine's voice-over than to her willingness to participate in the speech act.

WALLOWING IN A WALK-ON: CHRISTOPHER WALKEN AND THE "FERRARA MALE"

If **The Addiction**'s depictions of the (literally) fluid female body and its rejection of the polarities of speech can be considered through the work of Julia Kristeva, then it has ramifications for the casting of a male star such as Christopher Walken. Indeed, my rationale for choosing this film over its Walken-dominated companion piece **The Funeral** is that the latter's exploration of the dynamics between Ray and his near psychotic brother Chez occurs at the expense of the female characters depicted. Contrastingly, as **The Addiction** focuses almost entirely on its heroine Kathleen, it raises important questions about the role of the actor in works dominated by the complexities, contradictions and indeed resistances of female sexuality to the symbolic.

I have argued elsewhere that such abject female representations are complicated by their placement in the films of Abel Ferrara. Although his works frequently depict the woman's body as a source of violence and disgust, these definitions occur alongside a destabilizing of male sexuality.[20] It is precisely because the female body refuses its passive, violated status and frequently returns in a more disturbing form that it provokes both *verbalised* contempt and hysterical displays of aggression from the depicted Ferrara male. Once again, these elements of resistance occur not merely at the level of physiology, but also through a denial of discourse. These are heroines who are either unable to talk, as with Thana in **Ms.45** (1981) or turn to silence as a means of rejecting established speech patterns – as in the case of Kathleen and the nun who refuses to *name* her rapist in **Bad Lieutenant** (1992). This resulting loss of discourse frequently reduces the male to characteristically "feminine" displays of hysteria, suffering and exhibitionistic display.

If these depictions point to gaps in the secure "adult" construction of the male, then it extends beyond the content of Ferrara's films to include their actual casting. In particular, the director has repeatedly made a pointed use of actors whose performance style also exhibits certain tensions in both speech and sexual identity. In the figure of Harvey Keitel for instance, Ferrara has clearly found an actor willing to import a pained and failed vision of male subjectivity into his roles in films such as the **Bad Lieutenant** and Eddie Israel of **Dangerous Game** (1993). While it can be argued that Keitel has used his roles for Ferrara as a means of working through a set of very personal and emotional traumas, this has resulted in a style of performance which oscillates wildly between accentuated gestures of "adult" male aggression and infantile wailing and inarticulate utterances.

Thus to call the acting style of the Ferrara male as excessive or "melodramatic" requires an understanding that goes beyond theatrical method and seeks the basis of such performances in the infantile. To quote Elin Diamond, such works create:

.... the desire for a different performing body. Melodrama has offered complete adequation between the symptomatology of hysteria – eye-rolling, chocking, uncontrollable laughter – and the actor's verbal and physical signs... The hermeneutic pleasure... lay in its diminished gestural range, the presentation of the corporeal text riddled by gaps, feints, evasions.[21]

Although occupying a very different acting style to Keitel, Christopher Walken has also been noted as bringing a similar degree of emotional intensity and introspection to his roles for Ferrara. As Nick Johnstone has noted in his recent book *Abel Ferrara: The King Of New York*, the frequent casting of Walken is:

... proof that Ferrara has established himself as a director capable of extracting searing performances from established acting names. This is particularly true of Ferrara's use of Walken, an actor who has seemed cold in films where he hasn't connected with the director.[22]

Once again, the intensity which Walken displays in these works exhibits tensions around a secure vision of masculinity, pointing to a more infantile and decentred conception of the self. Indeed, although prone to psychotic outbursts and overblown displays of violence in his roles, Walken's slender frame and frequently high pitched and faltering vocal delivery lack even the physical bulk and ballast that Keitel uses to bolster an otherwise flagging filmed machismo.

Added to the tensions around masculinity implicit in the actor's appearance and delivery are those relating to the frequent off-screen projects which Walken is involved in. For instance, Ferrara has frequently talked about the pair's interest in adapting the story of 1970's male porn star John Holmes from Walken's own screen-play. As the director has stated "It's Chris's take on that person and being an actor and being famous and having a special gift and seeing where it can take you."[23] Holmes' performance "style" conflated a variety of signifiers around excessive masculinity (via his oversized phallus) within a distinctly pre-pubescent and asexual body shape that closely resemble Walken's slight frame. (Indeed the fact that Holmes' penis graced both heterosexual and gay porn scenarios adds to the chain of sexual ambiguity).

If the tensions existing in the construction of the "Ferrara male" mark a process of feminisation, then they are clearly present in Walken's brief role in **The Addiction**. Here, he is depicted (with a distinctly feminine hairstyle) as the vampire Peina, whom Kathleen initially stalks as a potential victim. After immediately recognising her addiction as that of the undead, Peina escorts her back to his apartment where he claims to be able to "train" her to control her addiction. In this respect, Walken's diegetic introduction as well as his brief "training" session with Taylor can be seen as coming at central point in the narrative. It occurs during the heroine's increasing isolation from the realm of logic, language and the speech-bound mediation of her doctoral thesis.

Indeed, even before Kathleen's infection, Ferrara clearly makes a series of parallels between vampiric addiction and other forms of "power based" obsession such as speech. It is intimated that Kathleen is already being controlled by the "rhetorical pusher" that is her college professor (Paul Calderon). This is a character who is revealed as couching debates in morality, evil and human existence as a precursor to student seduction. Although vampirism allows Kathleen to subvert existing power principles that such male characters hold over her (she first taunts, seduces and then infects her tutor), Nick Johnstone has argued that the professor's role as "educator" is replaced by that of Peina:

Until he takes his coat off Peina has been standing there lecturing her with his book still in his hand. This was Kathleen's world: books, knowledge, education and learning. Now she has a vampire professor who lectures her as her professor-boyfriend did.[24]

While the connections Johnstone makes between the two male characters in the film are persuasive, they fail to recognise the very different sets of influences that each brings to the heroine. Whereas the professor attacks Kathleen with a battery of rigid linguistic labels and philosophical terms, Peina introduces a set of creative references: discussing writers such as Beckett and Burroughs. In their unconventional fictional works, these authors render language ambiguous, collapsing the purity of the word into the dirt that is the uncontrollable infantile body.

In his brief training session with the heroine, Walken shifts from being the Ferrara male to fe-male. He emulates the role of the mother who trains (and restrains) the infant's body as well initiating the semiotic form of communication which the symbolic attempts to smother. It is only after her meeting with Peina that Kathleen is able to finish her doctoral thesis and fully jettison the realm of established language and physical representation. As her final monologue discloses: "To face what we are in the end, we stand before the light and our true nature is revealed. Self revelation is the annihilation of self".[25] The annihilation of self to which **The Addiction** ultimately refers, is the one in which body and sexual identity are mediated through the repressive structures of speech.

Xavier Mendik is a Lecturer in Media and Popular Culture at University College Northampton. He is completing a volume on Joe D'Amato entitled *Bodies Of Desire And Bodies In Distress* and is co-editor of *Violated Bodies: Images Of Pain*.

NOTES

1. Elizabeth Grosz (on the work of Julia Kristeva); *Volatile Bodies: Towards A Corporeal Feminism* (Bloomington: Indiana University Press, 1994), pp.193–194.

2. For an overview of the star studies debates and their development against auteur theory and its privileging of the director as the key creative source of film production, see Paul McDonald's chapter "Star Studies" in Joanne Hollows and Mark Jancovich (eds) *Approaches To Popular Film* (Manchester: Manchester University Press, 1995) pp.79–99.

3. These are outlined in Nick Johnstone, *Abel Ferrara: The King Of New York* (London: Omnibus Press, 1999), pp.112–123.

4. See Gavin Smith "Dealing With The Now" in Nick James (ed), *Sight And Sound* (April, 1997). Here Smith discusses the film as one example of Ferrara's interest in creating "introspective and claustrophobic" texts (p.4).

5. For instance, Rob White's *Sight And Sound* review of the film (April, 1997) noted: "Kathleen's vampirism coincides with her increasing immersion in continental philosophy and literature. For every blood-drinking set piece there's a classroom scene, or a discussion between Kathy and a teacher or fellow student, about European ideas" (p.40).

6. For an overview of these accounts see the chapter "The Performance Of Culture: Anthropological And Ethnographic Approaches" in Marvin Carlson, *Performance: A Critical Introduction* (London: Routledge, 1996), pp.13–34.

7. Paul McDonald, "Star Studies", p.86.

8. See Julia Kristeva, *Desire In Language* (New York: Columbia University Press, 1980).

9. Elin Diamond, "The Shudder Of Catharsis" in Andrew Parker and Eve Kosofsky Sedgwick (eds) *Performativity And Performance* (London: Routledge, 1995) p.153. It is interesting to note that the subversion of established (adult) modes of language is also central to Finley's work. In particular, Diamond notes two ways in which this artist emphasises the mouth as an orifice through which speech can no longer be transmitted. Firstly, through the application of foods to her body and face, Finley emphasises the mouth as a "shitting" orifice through which excremental substances rather than discourse flow. Secondly, it has been noted how Finley often transforms her voice into a grotesque gateway through which unidentifiable screeches, grunts and gurgling sounds can pass.

10. Roger Ebert, *The Addiction* (review) *The Chicago Sun-Times*, 10/27/1995 (p.1).

11. This is underscored by the fact that Kathleen's first victim is a male vagrant whom she attacks while he slumbers in a filthy alleyway. The fact that the heroine extracts the victim's blood with the use of a hypodermic needle reiterates the theme of vampire as junky that Ebert and others see as running through the film.

12. In terms of Kristeva's equation between disgust and the infantile world, it seems pertinent that Ferrara even connects the real-life horrors of the death camps to the realm of the child. For instance, in one sequence (the already infected) Kathleen is depicted wandering around an

exhibition devoted to the holocaust. Here, the camera shifts between shots of a small boy obsessed with the image of mass corpses which confronts him to that of a girl's doll which remains prominent in a collection of concentration camp memorabilia.

13. See Julia Kristeva, *Powers Of Horror: An Essay In Abjection* (New York: Columbia University Press, 1982).

14. Elizabeth Grosz, *Volatile Bodies: Towards A Corporeal Feminism*, p.192.

15. The fact that **The Addiction** focuses on "female blood" lust, rather than the figure of a male vampire also carries resonances relating to Kristeva's analysis. This is because she identifies waste matter as carrying degrees of impurity which relate to whether they are derived from the male or female body. As Grosz has noted in her review of Kristeva's work, the cultural distinctions which separate male from female body fluids further evidences language's ability to differentiate power in favour of the masculine. Its effect is seen in the example of the cultural status of semen. Although this is a "body product" Grosz suggests it is largely seen as a positive and "non-polluting" substance because of the "natural" qualities that sperm is seen to possess. Contrastingly, menstrual blood which, although a necessary process for procreation, carries largely negative cultural connotations, through its equation with wounding, death and sin (the longstanding myth of the female "curse").

16. The infantile associations of the orgy are underscored when Katherine is found wandering the streets wailing "mama" following her excess of feeding.

17. Grosz, p.194.

18. Rob White, p.40.

19. If the film views the act of vampirism as upturning established gender definitions of the feminine, then it is significant that following her infection Kathleen exhibits far more masculine attributes. Not only does her vicious assault on the ghetto youth "Black" (Fedro Starr) evidence her increased physical strength, but she is also referred to as "Kat", an abbreviation which points to her feline and unrestrained animalistic qualities.

20. See my article "Thana As Thanatos: Sexuality And Death In **Ms.45 Angel Of Vengeance**" in Andy Black (ed) *Necronomicon Book 1* (London: Creation Books 1996), pp.168–177. This work considers the heroine's body as open to duel physical and verbal attacks from the men depicted in the film. That Thana is depicted as both an object of desire and abject disgust in the narrative, points to the insecurities in male sexuality which necessitate such contradictory female constructions. For a further discussion of Ferrara's contradictory male representations see also my introduction to the *Visual Films* DVD release of **The Driller Killer**.

21. Elin Diamond, "The Shudder Of Catharsis", pp.157–158.

22. Nick Johnstone, *Abel Ferrara: The King Of New York*, p. 26.

23. Ibid., p.35.

24.. Ibid., p.173.

25. Cited in Johnstone, p.179.

'SUICIDE KINGS'

That phone call I got, it comes from outside high walls and fancy gates. It comes from a place you know about maybe from the movies. But I come from out there and everybody out there knows everybody lies. Cops lie, newspapers lie... The one thing you can count on? Word on the street. That's solid.

(Christopher Walken as Charles Barret)

Not even the most rabid Christopher Walken fan would claim that **Suicide Kings** (1998) is by any means the best of his movies. Even the copywriter for the UK video release couldn't be bothered to check that the name of Walken's character, calling him Charlie Bennet instead of Barret (and spelling Bennet two different ways on the sleeve). But that doesn't mean it's not worth the 102 minutes of your life it takes to watch it.

Above all else, Walken is a movie star who has achieved iconic status playing men who might just be capable of anything. At any time. Sometimes for the sheer hell of it. Think of the violence of his character in **King Of New York** for the classic example. See Walken walk into the frame and the weight of his career walks on with him. Like it or not (and there's plenty of interview evidence to suggest the actor might at least like to get offered the odd screwball comedy or Jane Austen adaptation), Christopher Walken is as much the personification of gangster cool as James Cagney was before him.

Typecasting? Well, yes, but typecasting that Walken doesn't shy from using to his own advantage. How many other actors could spend most of a movie stuck to a chair with gaffer tape yet still be the personification of barely restrained menace, especially an actor who acknowledges that one of his trademarks is to work a little jig into every part. Yet that's precisely what Walken does in this, a comparatively low budget ($5 million) tale of rich kids kidnapping a mobster.

Of course, this knowing toying with screen-image is fraught with danger. It's a technique that Clint Eastwood, for instance, came a cropper with when he both directed and starred in **Pale Rider**. In a dry run for **Unforgiven**, Eastwood attempted to redefine The Man With No Name by playing The Preacher, a gunslinger turned man of the cloth with a mysterious past and his own code of honour, a man steeped in violence who is trying to atone for his past. It backfired precisely because the film wasn't strong enough to untangle itself from Clint's spaghetti heritage.

In contrast, **Suicide Kings**, from first-time director Peter O'Fallon[1], largely avoids this trap with Walken's character. Apparently out of the mobster business, or at the very least claiming to be, Charles Barret is an ambiguous figure – his real name is Carlo Bartolucci, a name he is trying to leave behind because of its mobster connotations – but as the film unfolds we gradually get to know enough about him to make him plausible. Or as plausible as any Godfather character can be since Quentin Tarantino perfected his ironic take on gangsterdom.

Indeed, Tarantino is an inescapable reference point here from almost the moment the film begins. While **Suicide Kings** eschews Tarantino's trademark flashback structure (much imitated in movies such as Steven Soderbergh's Elmore Leonard adaptation **Out Of Sight**), much of the dialogue is heavy on the irony and draws attention to tiny, apparently insignificant details.

INSIDER DEALINGS

The opening scenes feature Walken as Charles Barrett strolling into a swanky bar where he is obviously a regular. Elegantly dressed, he goes to take his regular table, only to find that a group of rich kids are sitting there. Drawn into conversation, he agrees to go to dinner with them. "It's been a long time since I've been with guys," he remarks.

Trouble is, the guys – Henry Thomas as Avery Chasten, Sean Patrick Flanery as Max Minot, Jay Mohr as Brett Campbell and Jeremy Sisto as TK[2] – see Barret as a bargaining chip. Avery Chasten's sister Elise (Laura Harris) has apparently been kidnapped and the guys want some leverage over the kidnappers. Unable to come up with the $2 million it will take to pay the ransom, they want Barret to organise her release through his "contacts", and so kidnap him. As a token of their seriousness, they cut off his little finger.

"You're right, there was a time I could have done something," he tells them. "These days I'm a businessman. I pay my taxes like your moms and dads too." Brett, the most violent of the young man see things differently. "Once a criminal always a criminal. That's what my dad says," he notes.

The irony of his words, this little rich boy standing over a kidnapped man in danger of bleeding to death, is apparently lost on him. But then, it's a central tenet of this film that its morality is somewhat mixed up. Charlie may be a gangster, retired or otherwise, but he's infinitely more likeable than his Ivy League captors, something Walken himself has acknowledged. "Charlie is definitely something new," he said. "I think he's a good guy. I like him."[3]

In contrast, the kids who have captured him are a bunch of spoilt brats. Max, handsome if you liked Don Johnson in *Miami Vice*, is too obviously aware of his own good looks; TK is a medical student with a narcotics problem; Brett is a control freak who gets altogether too much of a thrill from pointing a gun; and Avery Chasen, despite a surface veneer of shy charm, turns out to be deeply flawed and weak.

Despite this, Barret, a man who has cheerfully snuffed people out in the past, is curiously drawn to his kidnappers. "He feels for them in the course of sitting there with them so intimately," noted Walken. "They do seem to get a kick out of each other in a strange way. I have it happen a lot. I look at young people and say, 'Gee I remember those days, it'd be fun to do that again.' I think that's why he sits down with them in the first place. He's out and wants to talk to young people. He's tired of talking to geezers."[4]

But even tied to a chair, drugged to the eyeballs with painkillers and missing his little finger, Barret is more than a match for these kids. He is being held at the home of their friend Ira Reder (Johnny Galecki)[5]. Ira is a man torn. Unaware of what the other four were planning, he was expecting an evening of poker and beer. It's immediately obvious why the others have kept him out of their plans. Ira, the geeky, bespectacled one of the group, veers between being worried that he's got a kidnapped gangster in his home and fearful that his parents will come home to discover the house in a mess. He's even worried that his friends are drinking his father's liquor, as his old man has marked the bottles.

Gradually, a strange bond develops between Ira and Barret. It's diametrically opposed to the scenario where kidnappers start to identify with their victims. Instead of a Patty Hearst scenario where the captive identifies with and eventually supports the kidnappers, Ira starts to seek Barret's approval as a way of deflecting criticism from his friends. "You're the man, Ira," says Barret. Ira, meanwhile, has to stop himself from calling Charlie "Sir". The scene where Ira and Charlie first come face to face neatly encapsulates Ira's neuroses. "Why is this man here?" Ira asks. "Why is he taped to my father's favourite chair?"

Having secured an ally of sorts, Barret works on the other members of the group. "I bet it seemed like a good idea when you were cooking it up, huh?" he says to TK, a medical student who is responsible for keeping the de-pinkied Barret from bleeding to death. "It's different up close and personal. Rich kid, you don't have the stomach for this kind thing. The drugs help, right? They make you brave."

Again, the contrast is explicit. Charlie is genuinely brave, or at least genuinely sadistic and not scared to use violence. This is made clear in a flashback scene showing Barret during the 1970s. Dressed like an extra from **Saturday Night Fever**, we see Charlie as a younger man, out strutting his stuff. We also see the violence he is capable of inflicting. When prostitute Lydia (Laura San Giacomo) is abused by her pimp for buying a pair of boots instead of passing on the money, Barret takes horrifically direct action by killing the pimp in cold blood. The fact that he does this in the toilet of a crowded bar is evidence that Barret can transgress against simple things like

homicide laws with virtual impunity.

It's therefore not surprising that Barret appreciates (and manipulates) the dynamics of his crazy situation much more clearly than his kidnappers. The rich kids are in over their heads, unable to think beyond the kidnapping. This is underlined when Barret needs to communicate with the outside world to try to find Avery's sister. He asks to use the telephone, but this causes an argument about whether Barret should be allowed to talk to anyone. "You didn't really think this through too good, did you?" Barret dryly notes. Ira's house, always filmed in a dark, claustrophobic manner and protected by a security firm who at one point send a guard around after an alarm goes off, has become a metaphor for the way the kidnappers themselves are cloistered, cut off from those sections of society who don't share in their privileges.

OUTSIDE IS SOCIETY
Barret, however, is at home outside. The outside world is brought into sharp relief by Barret's lieutenant and bodyguard Lono Veccio. Played by Dennis Leary in full-on wisecrack mode, Veccio is effectively Barret before he changed his name and tried to become respectable. He's also a psychopath who beats a man with a golf club to extract information.

Yet, as with Barret, we are also invited to sympathise with him. Veccio's background story is similar to that of Bud White (played by Russell Crowe) in **LA Confidential**. Physically abused by his father as a child, Veccio is happy to use violence, but only within a self-imposed code. A major transgression against this code is violence against women. In an echo of Barret's protection of Lydia, Viccio beats up the stepfather of a hostess who has given him information about who Barret was with at the bar. Just to underline Veccio's innate violence, he uses a toaster to inflict the beating.

More worryingly, however, we are also invited to identify with both Veccio and Barret because their self-reliance is diametrically opposed to that of Barret's captors. At one point, for instance, Barret is told to listen to TK's advice about not drinking alcohol because TK's "father is a doctor".

Contrast this with a scene where Veccio gives a wad of cash to a street person. The man is trying to make a few dollars cleaning windscreens, armed with a mop and "busket" (bucket). Veccio sees his gift as a way for the guy to get off the booze and off the streets. "If I see you in the streets again with a busket, I'm going to fucking shoot you," Veccio tells the man. The chance to change has been offered; it's up to the street person either to take it or face the consequences.

In short, we're offered two corrupt (and corrupting) visions of the world. The choice is simple. Which is more admirable? A privileged background where mother and father provide opportunities that their children either spurn or take for granted? Or a violent life where at least actions have direct and tangible, if sometimes terrible, results?

It's not much of a choice and you're naturally drawn towards Barret and Veccio because at least they have a twisted kind of integrity, but then again this is a perennial problem with mainstream gangster flicks. Different directors have come up with different solutions. As long ago as 1938, Michael Curtiz (who went on to win an Oscar for **Casablanca**) found a solution of sorts in **Angels With Dirty Faces**. In one of the classic Hollywood gangster movies, James Cagney as Rocky Sullivan becomes a hero to local kids. Going to the electric chair to pay for his life of crime, he fakes fear so that they won't follow in his footsteps. The solution is a fudge, a way of keeping the audience's sympathy with star Cagney, while also ensuring that conventional morality (crimes must be punished) wins out.

You might expect more recent gangster films to be more sophisticated, but even Francis Ford Coppola's **Godfather** trilogy ends with the entire Corleone family being massacred after we've been invited to witness Michael Corleone trying to sever his connections with organised crime. (Here, the Catholic Church is used a symbol of establishment corruption.)

One of the few gangster films to really get to grips with this issue is Martin Scorsese's **Goodfellas** (and the best gangster films that have followed, such as **Donnie Brasco**, owe Scorsese a debt for this). In **Goodfellas**, we are rarely invited to sympathise with the mobsters. All the main protagonists, Robert De Niro, Ray Liotta and Joe Pesci are despicable men. Any code of honour they have is really one of expediency: a code that they fervently hope will let them to make a dollar, stay tight with their bosses, and just stay alive to see another day.

If sentimentality and realism have been two ways to solve the dilemma of audience identification with gangsters, a third was brought into the mainstream by Quentin Tarantino with **Reservoir Dogs** and **Pulp Fiction**. It's been said many times before in different ways, but both are movies that are as much about other movies as they are about the characters we see on screen.

As noted before, it's this post-modern, ironic take that **Suicide Kings** so desperately wants to ape.[6] Sadly, the script just isn't up to the job. It's not the one-liners that are the problem. Much of the film is funny and sharply observed. Leary as Veccio, in particular, gets some great lines. "My fucking wife. I'm sure she used to have nipples that would stand up and whistle Dixie," he remarks to a sidekick, "but then again at one point dinosaurs used to roam the Earth."

Contrast this with the McDonalds/Burger King conversation in **Pulp Fiction**. There, when Vincent Vega (John Travolta) tells Jules Winnfield (Samuel L Jackson) about how they call a Big Mac "Le Big-Mac" in France, it's not only very funny, but we're also given some clue as to how stupid these men really are. This point is emphasised when Vega and Winnfield are forced to dress in geeky t-shirts to clean up a bloody mess.

Whatever way you look at it, **Suicide Kings** is never that subtle.

ANGRY BOYS

Yet, despite that, **Suicide Kings** is always watchable. If there are problems with the script (and a further criticism is that the script is too linear with flashbacks signposted so that the film is never as unsettling as it obviously wants to be), the performances here make up for a lot. As well as Walken, genuinely menacing, the young cast alongside him rise to the occasion.

In part, according to director O'Fallon, this was due to Walken's very presence. "First day of shooting, [Walken] shows up early on the set, earlier than anybody else," O'Fallon remarked in an interview to promote the film. "There's all these hot young stars in the film with him, and they show up late. They're 20-somethings who've been out partying all night. They're not serious and they're not ready for work. Chris sits down in a chair, puts one piece of tape on himself, so he can feel what it's like to work with his arms tied down. He's got a script and every line in it has a note next to it. He has a tape recorder that he's using to practice his lines aloud, to make sure they sound right. All these casual kids look at that and the next day they're there on time. They've all got notes."[7]

Perhaps as a result of this, there are moments when the scenes set in Ira's house truly crackle. While the cast may be comparative unknowns (although ironically Jay Mohr was a *Saturday Night Live* regular who used to do impersonations of Walken talking in his... trademark... slowly... punctuated... manner as part of his act), they never seem overawed by Walken.[8] Instead, they play off him, further allowing Walken's character to anchor the movie.

Such subtleties are needed because, as well as taking some of its moves from gangster movies, **Suicide Kings** (perhaps inevitably with its low budget) is also a film with many parallels to claustrophobic dramas of mistrust such as **Twelve Angry Men** or **The Treasure Of The Sierra Madre**. If key scenes set in Ira's house hadn't been convincing, the whole film would have completely failed.

However, it's not until it becomes obvious that the kidnapping of Chasten's sister must have been an inside job that Barret is really able to work on his captors. With the situation growing ever tenser, Barret draws the five into sitting with him and playing poker. "If I don't bleed to death pretty soon, I'm gonna die of boredom. How about we kill time instead?" he says. Ironically, Barret gets to spend quality time with the guys after all. You suspect that, deep down, he's quite enjoying himself.

With everyone together in the same room playing cards, he can play them off against each other, trying to discover who would have been desperate enough to agree to let Elise Chasten (one of their own after all – and these are very class-conscious young men) be kidnapped. And, if the metaphor of everyone playing poker together is somewhat clichéd then it's also forgivable because, as Barret discovers what's really going on, it's a genuinely chilling scene.

By the time he is through playing these rich kids off against each other, graphically showing them that their money will only buy them the illusion of control, the situation has completely changed. "You want to play?" he eventually asks. "Good, now we play my way." In truth, they've been playing things Charlie's way right from the beginning.

NOTES

1. Although this was Peter O'Fallon's first feature, he brought considerable experience from television, having directed episodes of, amongst other shows, *thirtysomething*, *Northern Exposure* and *Profiler* – all big hits Stateside.

2. All of the "guys" are comparative unknowns. Even Henry Thomas, who probably had the strongest track record prior to **Suicide Kings**, is best known for his part, while still a child, as Elliot in Spielberg's **ET**. Since then, he has hardly set Hollywood alight, although his credits include the hit TV series *Murder One*, the sci-fi mystery **Fire In The Sky** and the dreary epic **Legends Of The Fall**. Sean Patrick Flanery played *Young Indiana Jones* in the TV series spin-off from Spielberg's movies; Jay Mohr was primarily known for *Saturday Night Live*; and Jeremy Sisto's biggest film credit prior to **Suicide Kings** was the teen comedy **Clueless**.

3. Quoted from interview by Michael Kurcfeld.

4. Quoted from interview by Michael Kurcfeld.

5. Johnny Galecki was a regular as David Healy on *Roseanne* from 1991-97.

6. The script was by Josh McKinney, Gina Goldman (producer of *The Wonder Years*) and Wayne Allan Rice (**Only You**). It was based on a story called "The Hostage" by Don Stanford. Stanford scripted the wonderfully named B-movie **Monster A-Go-Go** (1965).

7. Quoted from interview by Roger Moore.

8. Walken has said in several interviews that he enjoyed Mohr's impersonation of him, although he did ask him not to do the impersonation on set.

A CHRISTOPHER WALKEN FILMOGRAPHY

Me And My Brother (1968)
The Anderson Tapes (1971)
The Happiness Cage (*aka* The Demon Within, 1972)
Next Stop, Greenwich Village (1976)
Annie Hall (1977)
Roseland (1977)
The Sentinel (1977)
The Deer Hunter (1978)
Last Embrace (1979)
Heaven's Gate (1980)
The Dogs Of War (1980)
Pennies From Heaven (1981)
Shoot The Sun Down (1981)
The Dead Zone (1983)
Brainstorm (1983)
A View To A Kill (1985)
At Close Range (1986)
Deadline (1987)
Homeboy (1988)
Biloxi Blues (1988)
Cannon Movie Tales: Puss in Boots (1988)
The Milagro Beanfield War (1988)
Communion (1989)
King Of New York (1990)
The Comfort Of Strangers (1990)
McBain (1991)
Batman Returns (1992)
Mistress (1992)
All-American Murder (1992)
Wayne's World 2 (1993)
True Romance (1993)
Pulp Fiction (1994)
A Business Affair (1994)
Nick Of Time (1995)
The Addiction (1995)
Things To Do In Denver When You're Dead (1995)

The Prophecy (1995)
Search And Destroy (1995)
The Wild Side (1995)
Last Man Standing (1996)
The Funeral (1996)
Basquiat (1996)
Celluloide (1996)
Privateer 2: The Darkening (1996)
Ripper (1996)
Mouse Hunt (1997)
Suicide Kings (1997)
Excess Baggage (1997)
Touch (1997)
New Rose Hotel (1998)
Antz (1998)
Trance (1998)
Illuminata (1998)
The Prophecy II (1998)
Kiss Toledo Goodbye (1999)
Sleepy Hollow (1999)
Vendetta (1999)
Blast From The Past (1999)
Cast And Crew (1999)
The Opportunists (1999)

INDEX OF FILMS

Page number in bold indicates an illustration

DENNIS HOPPER *Jack Hunter (editor)*
MOVIE TOP TEN

DENNIS HOPPER One of the most talented but controversial actors of recent decades, almost as notorious for his off-screen hell-raising as he is for his roles in such powerful films as his self-directed **The Last Movie**, David Lynch's **Blue Velvet**, and Tim Hunter's **River's Edge**.

Jack Hunter (author of film studies *Inside Teradome* and *Eros In Hell*) has selected his own chronological Top Ten of Dennis Hopper's movies, which are analysed in illustrated, in-depth essays by some of the best cutting-edge film critics of today. The result is both an incisive overview of Dennis Hopper as an actor, and an anthology of films by some of the leading cult directors of recent decades such as Wim Wenders, Tobe Hooper, David Lynch, Tim Hunter, Henry Jaglom, Curtis Harrington, and Hopper himself.

Featured films include: **Night Tide, The Last Movie, Tracks, Speed, The American Friend, Out Of The Blue, Texas Chainsaw Massacre 2, Blue Velvet, Rivers Edge**, and **Paris Trout**.

DENNIS HOPPER
MOVIE TOP TEN

easy rider
blue velvet
the last movie
river's edge
out of the blue
paris trout
tracks
night tide
the american friend
texas chainsaw massacre 2

CINEMA   Trade paperback   1 871592 86 0   192 pages   169mm x 244mm   £12.95

HARVEY KEITEL *Jack Hunter (editor)*
MOVIE TOP TEN

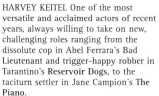

HARVEY KEITEL One of the most versatile and acclaimed actors of recent years, always willing to take on new, challenging roles ranging from the dissolute cop in Abel Ferrara's Bad Lieutenant and trigger-happy robber in Tarantino's **Reservoir Dogs**, to the taciturn settler in Jane Campion's **The Piano**.

Jack Hunter (author of film studies *Inside Teradome* and *Eros In Hell*) has selected his own chronological Top Ten of Harvey Keitel's movies, which are analysed in illustrated, in-depth essays by some of the best cutting-edge film critics of today. The result is both an incisive overview of Harvey Keitel as an actor, and an anthology of films by some of the leading cult directors of recent years, including Quentin Tarantino, Martin Scorsese, Nic Roeg, Abel Ferrara, Spike Lee, James Toback, and Jane Campion.

Featured films include: **Fingers, Mean Streets, Cop Killer, Bad Timing, Bad Lieutenant, Dangerous Game, Reservoir Dogs, The Piano, From Dusk Til Dawn**, and **Clockers**.

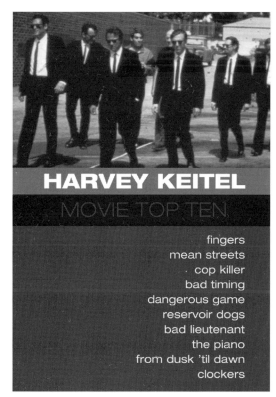

HARVEY KEITEL
MOVIE TOP TEN

fingers
mean streets
cop killer
bad timing
dangerous game
reservoir dogs
bad lieutenant
the piano
from dusk 'til dawn
clockers

CINEMA   Trade paperback   1 871592 87 9   192 pages   169mm x 244mm   £12.95

CREATION BOOKS

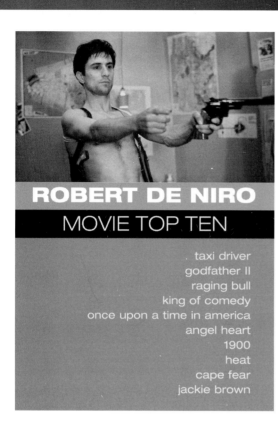

ROBERT DE NIRO *Jack Hunter (editor)*
MOVIE TOP TEN

ROBERT DE NIRO. One of the most versatile and acclaimed actors of recent years, famous for the uncompromising method approach he brings to roles ranging from the psychotic Travis Bickle in Martin Scorsese's seminal **Taxi Driver**, to the nerveless robber of Michael Mann's **Heat** and the loser in Tarantino's **Jackie Brown**.

Series editor Jack Hunter has selected his own chronological Top Ten of Robert De Niro's movies, which are analysed in illustrated, in-depth essays by some of the best cutting-edge film critics of today.

The result is both an incisive overview of Robert De Niro as an actor, and an anthology of films by some of the leading directors of recent decades such as Martin Scorsese, Michael Mann, Quentin Tarantino, Sergio Leone, Bernardo Bertolucci, and Francis Ford Coppola.

Featured films include: **Taxi Driver, Raging Bull, Angel Heart, Once Upon a Time In America, Jackie Brown, King of Comedy, Heat, 1900, Cape Fear, and Godfather II.**

ROBERT DE NIRO
MOVIE TOP TEN

- taxi driver
- godfather II
- raging bull
- king of comedy
- once upon a time in america
- angel heart
- 1900
- heat
- cape fear
- jackie brown

CINEMA   Trade paperback   1 871592 88 7   192 pages   169mm x 244mm   £12.95

JOHNNY DEPP *Jack Hunter (editor)*
MOVIE TOP TEN

JOHNNY DEPP. One of the most enigmatic and uncompromising actors of recent years, famous for a wide variety of movies ranging from Tim Burton's gothic fable **Edward Scissorhands** and lurid pulp movie tribute **Ed Wood**, to Terry Gilliam's psychedelic, paranoiac drug epic **Fear And Loathing**.

Series editor Jack Hunter has selected his own chronological Top Ten of Johnny Depp's movies, which are analysed in illustrated, in-depth essays by some of the best cutting-edge film critics of today. The result is both an incisive overview of Johnny Depp as an actor, and an anthology of films by some of the leading cult directors of recent decades such as Tim Burton, Jim Jarmusch, Terry Gilliam, John Waters, and Wes Craven.

Featured films include: **Edward Scissorhands, Donnie Brasco, Ed Wood, Cry-Baby, Fear And Loathing In Las Vegas, What's Eating Gilbert Grape, Nightmare On Elm Street, Platoon, Nick Of Time, and Dead Man.**

JOHNNY DEPP
MOVIE TOP TEN

- donnie brasco
- edward scissorhands
- fear and loathing in las vegas
- what's eating gilbert grape
- nightmare on elm street
- platoon
- nick of time
- ed wood
- cry-baby
- dead man

CINEMA   Trade paperback   1 871592 89 5   192 pages   169mm x 244mm   £12.95

CREATION BOOKS